President's Office
University of Illinois

Donated by

 Samuel K. Gove
Professor and Director *Emeritus*
Institute of Government
and Public Affairs

June 1988

The Washington Lobbyists
for Higher Education

The Washington Lobbyists for Higher Education

Lauriston R. King

Lexington Books
D. C. Heath and Company
Lexington,   Massachusetts
Toronto   London

Library of Congress Cataloging in Publication Data

King, Lauriston R
    The Washington lobbyists for higher education.

    Includes bibliographical references and index.
    1. Higher education and state—United States.
    2. Lobbyists—United States.   1. Title.
LC173.K5   379   74–25055
ISBN 0–669–96610–x

Published simultaneously in Canada

Printed in the United States of America

International Standard Book Number: 0–669–96610–x

Library of Congress Catalog Card Number: 74–25055

To Gerry,
Wife and Best Friend

Contents

List of Tables

Introduction

Prior to 1940 American higher education stood aloof from tough questions of politics and policy. Now, on a scale hardly imagined possible a short 20 years ago, the actions of the federal government impinge upon the conduct of higher learning. The roots of this transformation stretch back to World War II when the success of applied scientific research helped to hasten the defeat of the Axis powers.

Science had proved itself an invaluable national resource. Since much of the scientific research upon which these successes were based came from university-tied scientists, it was hardly surprising that science became synonymous with university science. Shortly after the end of the war, Edward C. Elliott, president emeritus of Purdue University, wrote of the new pressures for transformation in American higher education, particularly those tied to the scope and methods of scientific training and research. He observed that colleges and universities had been "brought into the arenas of large-scale organization and of politics. The freedom and financing of scientific advance are more than ever before likely to become entangled in the meshes of controversial public policy. . . . The process of successful reconversion to the new order of things will undoubtedly impose demands for new tactics on the part of educational and scientific leadership." [1]

In the intervening years, colleges and universities have been called upon to shelter and nurture the growth of an imposing science establishment. They have provided strategic redoubts from which activist students and faculty have launched assaults against a host of social and political problems ranging from civil rights to the Vietnam War. During the 1960s the elitist pretensions of American higher education have eroded in the face of public policies that urged them to embrace the very poor as well as the very rich.

The creation of permanent Washington offices by academic, institutional, and professional associations is one sign of the developing interest higher education has in maintaining and promoting its ties with government. This study explores this emerging relationship from the point of view of the Washington representatives for higher education, the men and women who staff the association offices, the offices of the various state systems of higher education, and the individual colleges and universities. It will describe who they are, who they represent, and the particular styles and values they bring to their profession. The objective is to look at the politics of higher education in Washington and place these findings in the wider setting of (1) the changing relationships between higher education and the federal government; (2) the emerging style of higher education in politics; and (3) the prospects for higher education in national interest politics. Higher education is treated here as a developing interest group, one that has clearly acknowledged stakes in the activities of the federal government, but which is still in the process of accommodating its political style and structure to the vastly expanded role that government plays in higher education.

Two basic considerations dictated the research strategy for the study of Washington representation. First, because one fundamental concern of the project was for broad institutional and political changes, it was necessary to find a point that was clearly indicative of the changing relationships between society, government, and higher education. Second, to document these changes in a concrete way it was necessary to narrow the focus to those persons most deeply concerned with and bound up in these changes. Consequently, the research centered on institutional representatives, those individuals in Washington offices representing colleges and universities, and not those from the occupational and functional groups and associations that are also component parts of the American higher education establishment.[2] Special task organizations like the National Commission on Accrediting, professional associations like the American Sociological Association, and the associations of individual members like the American Association of University Professors simply do not encompass the range and diversity of concerns, interests, and contacts with government that are characteristic of the colleges and universities themselves. Their political activities are limited and confined to the rather narrow concerns of their membership. More importantly, they lack the kinds of visible and sustained political involvement characteristic of the more inclusive institutionally-based associations and offices.

The criteria for the Washington representative of a higher education institution depended almost wholly upon titles within the office or association. Efforts were made to interview the executive chief of each office, most frequently designated the executive secretary, president, or director, and the person in charge of federal relations when the office or association supported such a division of labor. Fifty-nine men and women were interviewed according to these criteria. Although not everyone who could legitimately claim to represent higher education in Washington was interviewed, these 59 persons represent an extremely comprehensive cross-section of the capital's higher education community as it existed in late 1969 and early 1970, when most of the interviews took place. Additional interviews were conducted with a much smaller number of representatives during 1973 and 1974. In addition, approximately 25 interviews were conducted with present and former officials of the Department of Health, Education, and Welfare, professional lobbyists for labor and education, executives of individual membership groups and special task associations, and several observers particularly knowledgeable about higher education politics. The semistructured interviews ran from one-half hour to three hours in length, and included questions about the representatives' personal backgrounds; their relationships with their member institutions; the nature of their jobs; their views on the role higher education ought to play in politics; and their predictions about the kinds of changes likely to occur in the Washington higher education community during the coming years.

Many persons in Washington and at the University of Connecticut provided encouragement, criticism, and suggestions for this study. In Storrs, I owe a special debt of gratitude and appreciation to Everett C. Ladd, Jr., who first suggested developing the theme of the changing dimensions of knowledge and power in contemporary American society and politics. His unflagging energy and resourceful political imagination have provided continuing sources of admiration.

Once the topic was narrowed to the politics of higher education, I had the good fortune to discuss the subject with one of the most astute students and practitioners of education politics in the country, Homer D. Babbidge, Jr., former president of the University of Connecticut. It was at his suggestion that the research look at the then somewhat mysterious changes that were taking place in the Washington higher education community. He not only encouraged me to pursue the subject of Washington representation, but staked me to an exploratory trip to Washington to help get the project started.

Nearly all the Washington representatives gave generously of their time and thoughts. Several were kind enough to open their personal files to me so that I might get a detailed appreciation of the forces at work in the Washington higher education community. A number of the representatives, including John Talmadge, formerly with the Association of American Colleges, and John Crowley and Charles V. Kidd, both of the Association of American Universities, took time to read and comment on portions of earlier drafts, as did John C. Honey of Syracuse University and Donald Stewart of the University of Pennsylvania. My colleague and frequent collaborator, Philip H. Melanson of Southeastern Massachusetts University, also provided helpful comments and suggestions that were often bootlegged into the text without his knowledge.

In addition to the help provided by the representatives themselves, I also benefited from talks with a number of students, observers, and participants knowledgeable about the politics of higher education. E. Joseph Shoben, Jr., executive vice-president of the Evergreen State College in Washington, and Ian McNett, formerly with the *Chronicle of Higher Education,* offered incisive observations about the character of higher education politics. Dr. Weimer Hicks, president of Kalamazoo College, took the time to describe and document the relationship of the private liberal arts colleges to the Association of American Colleges. In addition, I benefited from discussions with several contributors to the small but growing literature on the politics of higher education, particularly as it is played in Washington. These included Harland Bloland of Columbia Teachers' College; Lawrence K. Pettit, commissioner of higher education, Helena, Montana; Lawrence Gladieux of the College Entrance Examination Board; and Thomas Wolanin of the University of Wisconsin, Madison. Larry Pettit generously let me use the manuscript copy of his study of the Higher Education Facilities Act of 1963, and Larry Gladieux and Tom Wolanin were kind enough to let me read several draft chapters of their case study of the passage of the Higher Education Amendments of 1972.

The actual research for the project would have been extremely difficult were it not for the generosity of the Connecticut Research Foundation and the National Science Foundation's program of dissertation research support. I gratefully acknowledge the support provided by these foundations.

At the National Science Foundation, Feenan D. Jennings, head of the Office for the International Decade of Ocean Exploration, has been a constant source of encouragement. I also wish to give special thanks to Cynthia Nash for her outstanding skill and unfailing good nature in preparing the manuscript for publication.

For some perplexing reason, wives always seem to come last in book acknowledgments. This hardly seems fair, especially if all wives are as patient and encouraging as my own. She never (openly) despaired that the book would get done. It is a pleasure and relief to find out that she was right—as usual—and to thank her once again.

Notes

1. Henry Herge, et al., *Wartime College Training: Programs of the Armed Forces* (Washington, D.C., 1948), p. 181.

2. Roger W. Heyns, "The National Educational Establishment: Its Impact on Federal Programs and Institutional Policies," *Liberal Education,* May 1973.

1 The Evolution of Federal Policy for Higher Education

Public Policy and Higher Education

Until Congress passed the National Defense Education Act (NDEA) in 1958, federal policy toward higher education was strictly a one-way affair in which government regarded the colleges and universities as resources for the solution of national problems. The institutions played a negligible role in shaping policies of direct benefit to themselves or their student constituents. Instead they willingly accommodated national policy by providing men and resources to carry out the objectives of the government. After 1958, however, federal policy toward higher education became more and more attuned to the overall place of education in American society, hence to the needs of institutions and students themselves.

Passage of the Morrill Land Grant Act of 1862 and subsequent legislation into the early 1900s firmly established the place of the national government in higher education.[1] Two significant precedents emerged from the Morrill Act that in many respects fixed the broad outlines of this relationship. First, the rationale for the act was based ostensibly on national needs for trained manpower in two specified fields of study—agriculture and mechanics. Second, the authorizing legislation did not require that the beneficiary institutions, or the institutions created as a result of the legislation, be public in support or control. Thus it served as a forerunner for all subsequent legislation in that it included both private and public institutions. Subsequently, when Congress has authorized federal programs it has made them available with few exceptions to both public and private colleges and universities.

Another spin-off from the land-grant acts was the creation of a formal organization to maintain contact between the schools. College representatives, dissatisfied with the sporadic contacts in the post-Civil War years, gathered in Washington in 1882 to discuss problems and policies. In 1887 they formed the Association of American Agricultural Colleges and Experiment Stations. From the time of its first meetings in 1882 and 1883 the new association was active in pushing federal legislation on behalf of its member colleges.

This emphasis on public, land-grant institutions reflected the heavily agricultural character of the national economy. Agricultural interests

1

promoted the kinds of institutions and services that were most compatible and advantageous to those drawing their sustenance from the land. While the private and denominational colleges tended the business of genteel and orthodox education for the nation's elites, the land-grant colleges and experiment stations brought practical knowledge and advanced training to more and more citizens. Along with the democratizing effects of the public colleges, the land-grant movement was important because it promoted the idea that advanced education could provide for social needs and public service, and not just for book learning in the classical tradition.

One significant political consequence of this notion of social utility was the development of a constituency (largely agricultural) and the heightened awareness by the land-grant colleges of their mutual interests.[a] They became increasingly attuned to the realities of political action, organization, and compromise. Creation of the association in 1887 and the active role played by its executive committee in drafting and promoting legislation that benefitted these schools marked the genesis of the national politics of higher education.

The powerful utilitarian strain in federal policy for higher education was buttressed by the experience of two world wars. Colleges and universities were enlisted in the national effort through campus military training, the creation of contractual relations between government and the universities, and the growth of federally sponsored research on campus. In 1916, with America still hanging back from the European war, Congress passed the National Defense Act, which reorganized the Army and for the first time created a system of military training in civilian schools and colleges, the Reserve Officers Training Corps (ROTC). This program was to help meet the Army's need for officers and to blunt the wholesale depletion of enrollments as students left for war. The outcome was the Student Army Training Corps, which was established at 525 colleges in 1918. It was disbanded that same year, shortly after the armistice.

The effects of these wartime programs on colleges and universities were limited because of the short time involved. They did, however, orient those in government and higher education toward the role that government could play in warding off potential financial disaster amidst wartime mobilization. Government contracts for military training served both the armed forces and the schools who feared that diminished enrollments would start a financial crisis. These programs brought college and university administra-

---

[a] Fed by a growing secondary school system that jumped from 1,026 public high schools in 1870 to 6,005 in 1900, and from 72,158 students to 519,251 during the same period, the state universities expanded rapidly. Between 1885 and 1895, for example, enrollments at eastern private colleges increased only 20 per cent, while those at state universities expanded by 32 per cent. John S. Brubacker and Willis Rudy, *Higher Education in Transition* (New York: Harper and Row, 1968), p. 161.

tors together with government officials on a more or less regular basis. One outcome was to blunt active efforts to promote policy on its own behalf because the main emphasis was on consultation and negotiation to iron out the details of the relationship. The character of this relationship was captured in 1918 by John H. MacCracken, president of Lafayette College. He suggested that American education was not organized to make its greatest contribution to the war effort and that there existed a need for both government and higher education to coordinate their efforts. He argued that

the government at Washington needs during the war an administrator of government of education. . . . His function will be to coordinate the demands made upon education by the government in the prosecution of war.

The colleges need a War Council. . . . This board ought to represent the colleges as distinct from the government, though in hearty sympathy and cooperation with it. It ought to have national representatives at Washington to give expression to any questions of national policy upon which the organizations represented may agree.[2]

Subsequently, representatives of seven national organizations concerned with higher education formed and approved the recommendation of Dr. Samuel P. Capen, of the Bureau of Education, for an Emergency Council on Education (later to be known as the American Council on Education), composed only of organizations and with the following objective:

The object of the Council is to place the resources of the educational institutions of our country more completely at the disposal of the national government and its departments to the end that through an understanding cooperation:

The patriotic services of the public schools, professional schools, the colleges and universities may be augmented;

A continuous supply of educated men may be maintained; and

Greater effectiveness in meeting the educational problems arising during and following the war may be secured.[3]

A second, but far less significant aspect of federal-collegiate relations involved contractual arrangements for training technicians in vocational training courses. About 95 college-level institutions received contracts under the "vocational" part of the program, of which about 20 were private and the remainder under the state and municipal control.[4]

In addition to military and technical training, the universities and colleges also contributed personnel and facilities for wartime research. In contrast to the post-World War II years, scientists left their universities to conduct research in government and industrial laboratories. What wartime research did take place at universities was staked not by federal dollars but by university or National Research Council funds derived from private foundations like Rockefeller and Carnegie. Most often a research project would be initiated at a university and supported by private funds. When some progress had been made or when the project became of sufficient interest to the government, the scientists would receive commissions and frequently move into government laboratories.[5] Research for wartime purposes had attained enough importance to be considered a part of the war effort, though certainly a minor part, and the universities were the source of research expertise to which government turned.

While the wartime crisis promoted substantially increased contacts between higher education and government, the relative tranquility of the interwar years diminished the federal role until the Depression. Several emergency federal programs were set up which affected higher education, the most significant one being a student work-study program administered by the National Youth Administration. Though limited, the program was important because it helped dispel the pervasive misgivings about federal control and replaced them with a growing opinion that the federal government could assist higher education by aiding students without untoward side effects.[6] The work-study program reflected the pattern of the government interest in higher education in that the program grew out of broad relief and employment policy and was not dictated by the need for federal aid to education.

In many respects the experience of higher education during the Second World War was similar to that of the First World War, but differed significantly in size and scope. Colleges and universities provided personnel and facilities for meeting critical manpower needs. For example, the Engineering, Science, and Management War Training Program conducted on the college campuses trained more than 1.5 million men and women in a wide variety of technical skills ranging from chemistry to drafting to production supervision. To bolster the shrinking supply of persons in engineering, physics, medicine, and pharmacy, Congress authorized $5 million for loans to students in these areas in 1942. Between 1942 and 1944 when the student loans were granted, over 11,000 students in 286 colleges and universities benefitted from the program. Enlisted men attended some 200 colleges and universities in the Army Specialized Training Program, which prepared them in engineering, linguistics, physics, mathematics, and medicine.[7]

The crowning piece of federal education policy during the war years was the Servicemen's Readjustment Act of 1944, the G.I. Bill of Rights. A fortuitous blend of patriotic, political, and economic motives helped design the law, which made it possible for over 2 million veterans to study at colleges and universities and nearly 3.5 million to study at schools below college level by 1955. Veterans' aid was good politics for President Roosevelt, who was seeking his fourth term, and of potential economic utility in reducing unemployment among the returning G.I.'s. The bill was pushed by veterans' groups like the American Legion, which argued the need for some national display of gratitude for the sacrifices of those who served in the armed forces.[8] Even though the G.I. Bill, and its successor, the Cold War G.I. Bill, (which further extended benefits to veterans who served in active duty after 1955) enabled millions of ex-servicemen to attend colleges, they were never seen as a sign of any federal commitment to equal educational opportunity. Rather, they were designed to compensate a particular category of persons for time away from normal civilian life, including the chance to pursue advanced education.

Again, it was the federal government that determined which programs were in the national interest, and it was the colleges that were the vehicles for their implementation. Wartime demands made it impossible for higher education either in good conscience or in good faith to press demands or interests of its own. The overall effect of this passive, cooperative style was to set a precedent that stretched well into the 1960s.

Yet the precedent did not mean a completely one-way relationship. It also involved a recognition on the part of the federal government that in using the resources of higher education it also had some responsibility for its welfare. The government found the resources of the colleges and universities invaluable in the war effort and enlisted all the major institutions as well as many of the smaller ones. Without the federal projects many of these schools would have been hard pressed to keep up their programs. It became a matter of federal concern that a number of the projects were openly or tacitly designed to make it possible, with federal assistance, for higher education to survive the period of low enrollments during the war.

It is perhaps inaccurate to refer to the relationship between higher education and the federal government as guided by a policy as such. Rather it was a relationship based on critical national situations and geared to the needs of a particular category of individuals or the research needs of the government agencies. There was a consistently instrumental view of education, a feeling that the colleges and universities of the nation were well equipped to do things that needed doing, whether training agronomists, helping to increase crop yields, or building a reserve of officers for the armed forces. Only since 1958 and the signing of the National Defense Education Act has the federal government started to turn away from this instrumental view of higher education to the kinds of policies that recognize that these institutions have needs and interests in their own right.

National Policy for Higher Education After 1958

The 1958 National Defense Education Act (NDEA) was important "not so much because of the specific provisions . . . but because of the psychological breakthroughs it embodied. It asserted, more forcefully than at any time in nearly a century, a national interest in the quality of education that the states, communities, and private institutions provide." [9] Although the ostensible federal interest in passing the eclectic measure was national defense, there was also some suggestion that the federal government was moving in the direction of guaranteed opportunity for higher education. The preamble to the law stated that "the security of the Nation requires the fullest development of the mental resources and technical skills of its young men and women. . . . The national interest requires . . . that the federal government give assistance to education for programs which are important to our national defense." [b]

To implement this goal the act included provisions aimed at correcting "as rapidly as possible the existing imbalances in our educational programs which have led to an insufficient proportion of our population educated in science, mathematics, and modern foreign languages and trained in technology." The key provisions provided grants to the states for the improvement of public school instruction in science, mathematics, and modern languages, and grants to colleges for teacher training institutes. It also provided for graduate fellowships for students anticipating a college teaching career.

The act stressed the relation between educational quality and the national interest in defense and security, but also recognized the need to find and educate talented individuals. Meeting this need required that there be an assurance that "no student of ability will be denied an opportunity for higher education because of financial need." No longer then was federal aid to students restricted to special skill groups like scientists or based on considerations other than educational benefit. This mix of instrumentalism and expanded federal aid to students was also reflected in the Higher Education Act of 1965. Lyndon B. Johnson's vision of the Great Society contained a sharply defined perspective on what education could do, both for the individual and for society. For example, the act contained a provision for community service and continuing education (Title I) that authorized

---

[b] The successful Soviet launch of Sputnik is often credited with having a powerful role in passing NDEA, but the ideas that went into the bill stretched back for several years. Sputnik merely provided the catalyst. Democratic Senator Lister Hill of Alabama made the Soviet exploit the vehicle for carrying an aid-to-education program through Congress. Following Hill's instructions, his staff put together a bill that linked education to defense and guided it "between the Scylla of race and the Charybdis of religion," and at the same time, pulled together the best ideas for education legislation afoot at the time. "In accepting the title 'national defense education act,' Hill observed that his colleagues would not dare vote against both national defense and education when joined in the same bill." James L. Sundquist, *Politics and Policy: The Eisenhower, Kennedy, and Johnson Years* (Washington, D.C.: The Brookings Institution, 1968), p. 176.

federal matching grants to the states to develop community service programs conducted by public or private nonprofit colleges and universities. The programs were to give special emphasis to urban and suburban problems, including housing, poverty, employment, transportation, health, and other local problems. Again the universities and colleges were called upon to assist the realization of national goals, this time during a peaceful interlude in the earlier ties of higher education and government.

At the same time the government worked to expand its assistance to students by taking the unprecedented step of providing federal scholarships for undergraduate students. These scholarships, "educational opportunity grants" (EOGs), were to be awarded by colleges to students of "exceptional financial need." Beyond this provision of funds, however, the act stipulated that colleges, in applying for scholarship funds, make an agreement with the commissioner of education to review each applicant's financial situation and set up programs to encourage able but needy high school students to attend college. Furthermore, it authorized the commissioner to make contracts with state, local, or private nonprofit organizations to identify and encourage needy high school students to attend postsecondary schools; to publicize existing student-aid programs; and to encourage capable high school and college dropouts to continue their education. In short, higher education was drafted into the offensive against poverty and, simultaneously, compelled to take steps to promote extensive social change.

Along with increased support to students, federal policy has provided increasing support for the institutions themselves. Such support has included grants and loans for facilities construction, "developing institutions," and specific facilities like libraries. Prior to 1963 and the passage of the Higher Education Facilities Act, the only significant policy toward the construction needs of colleges and universities was the 1950 Housing Act, which authorized 50-year, low-interest government loans to public and private colleges and universities for dormitory construction.

In one of his first messages to Congress in 1961, President Kennedy requested a program of federal loans for construction of college classrooms and other facilities. Throughout that year the House and Senate laid the groundwork for the bill, only to have it abruptly torpedoed by religious and political controversy during the next session.[10] In 1963 Kennedy focused his attention on construction loans to four-year undergraduate public and private institutions and grants for public junior colleges, two-year technical schools, college libraries, and public and private graduate schools. Subsequently, the Congress enacted the Higher Education Facilities Act of 1963 and authorized grants as well as loans to private nonprofit colleges but— to minimize the potential resurrection of the religious issue—specified that the grants could be used only for certain categories of facilities, such as science laboratories or classrooms for teaching mathematics.

The federal shift away from the instrumental view accelerated with passage of the Education Amendments of 1972.[11] They extended through fiscal 1975 the authorization for programs established by the Higher Education Act of 1965, the NDEA of 1958, the Higher Education Facilities Act, and the International Education Act. Although much attention to the bill was diverted by the acrimonious debate over the antibusing provisions attached to the bill, several provisions marked important breaks with earlier trends in federal policy toward higher education. Specifically, the bill authorized a restructured and greatly expanded system of federal subsidies to postsecondary students, a $1 billion-a-year grant program to aid colleges and universities, and an upgraded educational research program through a new National Institute of Education housed in the Department of Health, Education, and Welfare.

The most significant departure from earlier legislation was a specific federal commitment to provide all comers with a realistic opportunity for postsecondary education. This commitment is in the form of Basic Educational Opportunity Grants (BOGs) under which any college student in good standing is entitled to a basic grant less the amount his family can reasonably be expected to contribute toward his educational expenses. It is potentially the most extensive federal commitment to financing higher education since the G. I. Bill. Equally important, the 1972 amendments included a complex, formula-based program of direct institutional grants to colleges and universities with no strings attached. Institutional grants, unencumbered by federal restrictions on their use, had long been a goal of the major higher education associations.

The 1972 legislation marks a break with earlier federal policy for higher education in its stress on the accountability of colleges and universities for their stewardship of federal education programs and on the need for innovation and reform in higher education. Two students of education policy conclude that the amendments chart a new direction toward

a broadening of the scope of permissible federal action that is not seen to compromise the role of the states or to constitute "undue" federal interference or control; an evolution in the purposes sought by federal policy through higher education with equal educational opportunity now paramount; a movement from neutrality between public and private institutions to some preference for the privates; and the ascent of higher education toward a more co-equal status with elementary and secondary education in the federal concern for education.[12]

In spite of funding limits, the BOG and institutional grant provisions were explicit acknowledgements that the federal interest transcended the mere use of these human and institutional resources to attain national goals. In short, in less than 15 years this shift in federal policy has resulted in a commitment to help students get a college education as well as a commitment to the institutions themselves for building facilities to house and educate those seeking postsecondary education.

Higher Education and Big Science

The emergence of big science has probably done more than anything to alter the relationship between higher education and government.[c] The devastating atomic blasts that leveled Hiroshima and Nagasaki in the summer of 1945 gave stunning testimony to the power of American wartime scientific achievements. Imaginative basement inventors were displaced by organized, collective scientific efforts put together and funded by the government. Both Dr. Vannevar Bush's *Science, The Endless Frontier* (1945) and the five-volume study by the President's Scientific Research Board, *Science and Public Policy* (1945) recognized the impressive accomplishments of science during the war and urged that science be treated as a national resource. Growing tensions between the United States and the Soviet Union reinforced the view that the scientific and engineering manpower that developed nuclear weapons was crucial for maintaining national security.

The elevation of science to public prominence reinforced and elaborated the federal government's instrumental views of higher education. During the war, mobilization of university science was selective rather than general. Big contracts were concentrated in areas of direct military concern and most often went to schools that already had established research capabilities. Pressures of time, demands for secrecy, and the vast complexity and sophistication of modern warfare all conspired to make far-reaching distinctions within the scientific and technical communities. Of some 200 schools receiving a total of $235 million in research contracts from the government, 19 universities and institutes accounted for three-fourths of the total. And of nearly 2,000 industrial organizations receiving a total of almost $1 billion in research contracts from the government, fewer than 100 firms accounted for more than half the total.[13]

Thus, without plan or prospect, the university part of the higher education community became a partner in the new scientific estate. And with this new relationship arose political questions on matters of institutional

---

[c] Frederick Seitz refers to "big science" as that reflected in programs that require very large and costly items such as high energy accelerators, large astronomical observatories, oceanographic vessels, large nuclear reactors, and large rocket boosters. Frederick Seitz, "The University: Independent Institution or Federal Satellite," in Boyd Keenan, ed., *Science and the University* (New York: Columbia University Press, 1966), p. 157. The connotation here is much broader than Seitz's meaning, because it refers fundamentally to large-scale *publicly supported* science.

distribution of funds, the impact of federal dollars on the schools themselves, and the creation of a new clientele for the government funding agencies. The political impact of research and development money springs directly from the concentration of this money in a relatively few universities with extensive research programs. In 1972, for example, the first 100 universities and colleges accounted for 65 per cent of total federal funds to all institutions, a decline from the 69 per cent share held in 1971.[14] Obligations for such support, although declining, remain heavily concentrated in universities with powerful research traditions.

When this concentration of research money is viewed from the instrumental or problem-solving perspective of the government, government policy toward higher education is following a lengthy and consistent pattern. The major change has been in the magnitude and sustained character of this relationship after 1945. Because federally sponsored academic science is guided by research concerns, and to a large extent dominated by agencies whose objectives are not those principally associated with strengthening higher education, such support cannot in literal terms be considered an aspect of federal aid to higher education. If, however, such funds are regarded as financial patronage, or one indirect way of supporting higher education, then a whole cluster of political problems opens up.

The main problems come down to the equitable distribution of federal resources to institutions and geographic regions, and the impact of these funds on the programs and financial health of the schools themselves. The grip of a relatively few institutions on federal dollars has sparked at least a bit of envy, some very real financial dilemmas, and efforts to transform support for scientific research into more general federal aid to higher education. These problems are the special lot of the four-year liberal arts colleges and the rapidly growing number of community colleges. The dilemmas are compounded because the educational and financial problems of marginally participating academic institutions are not the result of federal support for academic science because such programs are geared specifically for the development of science and technology in the national interest.[d]

Not only has public science, primarily as carried on in American uni-

---

[d] One student concludes that the failure of federal funds to reach each and every institution should not provide the basis for attacking the existing system of distributing money for academic science. He suggests that "such criticism, especially the failure to give aid to the vast population of smaller and less affluent institutions, can only have validity if such aid were the prime objective of these funds. There has been a tendency to hold federal programs in support of science responsible for failures that could well be attributed to lack of local initiative and regional responsibility, and inadequacy of standards for educational programs." William Consolazio, *The Dynamics of Academic Science* (Washington, D.C. National Science Foundation, 1967), p. 13.

versities, helped generate a number of competing interests, but it has also raised the key question for higher education and government: What is the proper form of federal financial support to colleges and universities? Although research and development support has been geared toward hard results and not educational subsidies it has in many instances come to look like aid to institutions themselves. Such support can come in the form of fattened faculty paychecks, the purchase of costly equipment, or the construction of new buildings to house special research projects. Some major research universities have drawn an increasingly large share of their budget from federal funds. Four-year colleges, liberal arts schools, and community colleges have been deprived of these benefits and understandably have tried to promote more widespread and equitably distributed federal support for higher education. Federal support of science has provided an important model for these efforts.[15]

The final item linking potential political questions with public science and the universities is the crumbling of the local, parochial liberal arts college in the wake of the great research universities.[16] Increasingly, models for higher education are those schools that have acquired abundant renown and federal money as a result of their size and contributions to new knowledge. It is clearly not in the interest of disadvantaged or marginal institutions to admit publicly that government support for research is in fact the purchase of a service rather than support of higher education. Trapped between costs pushed inexorably upward by inflation, and the decreasing capacity of tuition, endowment, and alumni support to provide a sound financial base, it is wholly understandable that they should emphasize the role of federal dollars in developing the great national universities.

In a variety of ways the emergence of public science since 1945 has played a crucial part in defining the political agenda for American higher education. It pointed to potential new sources of support for higher education, created new constituencies, developed research in colleges and universities, and provided new or refined models of excellence and achievement. In the wake of these effects, however, public science prompted questions about the equitable distribution of resources, helped bring in new contenders for support, and new organizations and institutions to promote and referee the struggle to clarify and resolve these issues.

The Creation of an Institutional Framework

Changes in the higher education-government relationship resulted in the creation of new institutions and the renovation of old ones. The changes came fast, with few precedents in scale, complexity, or demands for specialized knowledge. New and altered institutions were politically significant because they provided visible links between campus administrators, their Washington agents, and the government machinery. Equally important, these institutions provided the framework within which the well-documented tendencies of both bureaucracies and their clients to keep programs well-funded and alive could take place, thus cementing mutually beneficial relationships.

Historically, the Office of Education (OE) has not provided a hospitable or effective institutional base for higher education. Only in recent years has the OE become responsible for managing and administering the higher education legislation of 1958 (NDEA), 1963 (Higher Education Facilities Act), 1965 (Higher Education Act of 1965), and the subsequent 1972 amendments. Congress chartered the Office of Education in 1867 to collect "such statistics and facts as shall show the conditions and progress of education in the several states and territories, and aid the people of the United States in the establishment and maintenance of efficient school systems, and otherwise promote the cause of education throughout the country."

The Office of Education held closely to this mandate until well into the 1950s when its activities were restricted mainly to the collection and dissemination of educational statistics and to technical consultation.

Aside from grants-in-aid for vocational education and to Land Grant Colleges under automatic, non-discretionary formulas, USOE managed next to nothing. It had few friends apart from the National Education Association, the American Association of School Administrators and the Council of Chief State School Officers, whose Washington staffs and whose constituencies found the statistical and advisory services of USOE of direct value. There was at least some validity to the widely held assumption that USOE was, in fact, the "kept" Federal agent of these major private educational associations.[17]

Higher education has never had much influence in the Office of Education, first because OE's main concerns have been for elementary and secondary education, and second because higher education itself saw few advantages in close ties with the office. Higher education's earlier obsession with "autonomy" and "government meddling" helped set the pattern for this relationship. Prior to World War I an office specialist on higher education set out to collect data to define what constituted a college or university. News of the study leaked to the press and ignited a nationwide furor among educators, who carried their efforts to suppress the report to President Woodrow Wilson. Wilson ordered the Office of Education not to release the report. During the next 30 years it became extremely hard for the office to obtain the cooperation of colleges and universities in gathering statistics on higher education.[18]

The almost complete impotence of the Office of Education on policy matters is reflected in the fact that the passage of key Johnson legislation in 1963 and 1964, including the Higher Education Facilities Act, the creation of the Office of Economic Opportunity, and the passage of Medicare, were due in large part to a few key appointments by HEW Commissioner Francis Keppel. These appointees, working mainly out of the Office of Program and Legislative Planning, set out to construct a coherent legislative policy that would avoid the problems that blocked the education legislation of the early 1960s. The important point here is "this legislative planning process worked as well as it did was a testament to the wisdom and ability of the participants rather than to any structured information base or long-range planning staff in USOE." [19] It was not until 1964, the year after passing of the Higher Education Facilities Act, that a new Bureau of Higher Education was set up to help administer the new higher education legislation.

The establishment of the National Science Foundation in 1950, the subsequent creation of an executive science apparatus, and the proliferation of science advisory committees in all branches of government also created points of access for the university part of higher education. University scientists were heavily represented on these committees, as well as in the former Office of Science and Technology, and the President's Science Advisory Committee (PSAC).

It would be fatuous to imply some kind of conspiratorial role among university scientists serving in advisory or official positions, but there does exist a perhaps unavoidable bias that identifies science with university science. Alvin Weinberg, former director of the Atomic Energy Commission's Oak Ridge National Laboratory, observed that

even the professor of purest intent must be in some measure loyal to the Estate which he represents. As a result, government scientific advisory circles tend to be preoccupied with science at the universities, rather than with science in industry or in government laboratories; the whole structure and cast of thinking is geared to the problem of university science, and the limitations of the university as an instrument of government are overlooked. *It would not be a great exaggeration to describe the advisory apparatus . . . as a lobby for the scientific university.*[20]

Early in 1973 President Nixon dismantled the entire top echelon of the federal science establishment by abolishing the post of science advisor, the President's Science Advisory Committee (PSAC), and the Office of Science and Technology. The ostensible reasons for the move were the president's determination to streamline the federal bureaucracy and limit the number of officials and advisers with direct access to him. Responsibility for scientific advice was shifted to the director of the National Science Foundation who was to report to one of the president's special assistants.

The impact of this reorganization on university science is not yet clear.

It does mean that scientists are further removed from the White House than at any time in the past decade, both in an actual and a symbolic sense. The existence of a formal, highly structured science advisory operation in the executive offices meant that university scientists had at least minimal access to policy makers in the Executive Branch.[e] It also helped increase the visibility of scientists who have been most frequently (and often inaccurately) identified as having university affiliations. Science in this setting almost invariably becomes·identified with the major and most prestigious universities in the nation. Higher education as a distinctive activity with interests and concerns going beyond natural and physical sciences becomes obscured and shunted aside in the press of these major national science policy issues.

The National Science Foundation is also a key part of the national science establishment, with important links to the academic world. The first point of contact is NSF's mandated responsibilities for science education in the country; the second the disproportionate number of university-affiliated scientists receiving NSF research support; and the third its role as science advisor to the president.

The foundation's relationship with higher education is not wholly one of financial patronage geared to improved science education. The men who serve on the policy-making arm of NSF, the National Science Board (NSB), as well as those who serve on the special advisory committees, come disproportionately from backgrounds in university science. Of the 88 members who have served on the NSB through mid-1974, 77 per cent (68) came from colleges or universities, 15 per cent (13) from industry, and 8 per cent (7) from foundations or other nonprofit organizations, such as the American Council on Education and the National Academy of Sciences. Again, this is not to argue that they are tools of the large research universities, or that they are so myopic as to identify the needs of these schools with the broader, more complex aspects of national science policy. Invariably, however, there will exist among men of comparable backgrounds who share similar views about the role of science and research a predilection that tends to identify science with science as it is carried on in the university as opposed to the industrial or government laboratory.

The structural setting for a politics of higher education is a relatively new phenomenon with important roots in the stunning growth of federal

---

[e] It took little over a year for the academic-scientific community to resurrect the issue of a presidential scientific advisory structure. See, for example, "Science and Technology in Presidential Policy-making—A Proposal," Report of the *ad hoc* Committee on Science and Technology, National Academy of Sciences (Washington, D.C., June, 1974); and U.S., Congress, House of Representatives, Committee on Science and Astronautics, *Federal Policy, Plans and Organization for Science and Technology,* 93rd Cong., 2nd Sess., 1974.

patronage for science, and, increasingly, through public laws geared more and more concretely toward the needs of higher education. The creation of the National Science Foundation in 1950 helped generate concern for science education as well as for the support of basic research. It also created an agency with direct contacts throughout the academic science community, many members of which staffed the administration of the foundation, and many more of whom helped pass on the desirability of granting their academic peers research money through the project grant system. In addition, the increasing number of institutional support programs has created a sufficient taste by colleges and universities for more funds unencumbered by categorical restraints.

In a less direct and programmatic way the science organization of the White House after 1958 was also, through its efforts to give some direction to American science, able to give some consideration and support to the institutions where most of the scientific research took place, the major universities. The science advisory structure also drew heavily for its staffing on scientists with stature and prestige in academic circles. It is wholly inaccurate to claim that the organization of big science can be equated with the political interests of higher education. That is simply not the case. All that can be said is that through the federal interest in science and the development of scientific manpower, higher education came into increasingly close contact with the federal government, and, more importantly, the power of federal money.

Paradoxically, the source of greatest payoff for higher education, the legislative process, is probably the least amenable structure in terms of its organization for developing fairly regular channels of contact and assistance.

Not surprisingly, the congressional structures for dealing with higher education are relatively new and committee jurisdictions diffused. For example, it was not until 1958 that the House authorized a standing Committee on Aeronautics and Space Sciences. In the House, seven of the 17 standing committees, plus seven subcommittees, deal with some aspect of higher education; in the Senate, five of 15 standing committees, plus seven subcommittees concern themselves with various higher education questions.

Program responsibilities are scattered all over. For example, the State Department educational exchange programs are the responsibility of the House and Senate Foreign Affairs and Foreign Relations Committees; the agriculture committees handle all business connected specifically with the land-grant colleges; and the Interstate and Foreign Commerce Committee of the House and the Labor and Public Welfare Committee of the Senate are responsible for the National Institutes of Health.

Formal responsibility for education rests with the House Committee on

Education and Labor and the Senate Committee on Labor and Public Welfare. The Senate, which still has no subcommittee confined to matters relating to higher education, did not create its education subcommittee until 1955. It was not until 1961 that the House Committee established the Special Subcommittee on Education with standing jurisdiction over higher education bills. During that year, Adam Clayton Powell, chairman of the House Education and Labor Committee, appointed an Advisory Group on Higher Education to study the needs of higher education and to delineate legislative priorities. Out of this group emerged a bipartisan bloc of moderates on the Education and Labor Committee who were able to coalesce around issues of federal support for higher education. Lawrence K. Pettit, in his account of the passage of the Higher Education Facilities Act of 1963, concludes that "Republicans and Democrats who traditionally have engaged in acrid ideological combat over both aid-to-education and labor issues were not able to formulate agreement on college aid signaled not only subtle and important changes respecting the Committee's modus operandi, but served also to delineate *higher* education as a separate policy area." [21] The 1962 emergence of this bipartisan bloc of college-aid advocates within the House Committee on Education and Labor was critical for education legislation. It was characterized by a moderate style that emphasized consensus on higher education and that became identified within the committee as an influential group willing to place a high priority on college-aid legislation.[22]

The higher education legislation passed after 1958 resulted in a fundamental transformation in the relations between the federal government and the nation's colleges and universities. There has been a steady move away from narrow purpose support of specified groups or activities deemed in the national interest to the broad federal support of both students and institutions. Along with this orientation toward higher education has come an increasingly large and complex network of institutions, organizations, and individuals that are involved in cementing these new relationships.

At the same time, however, the consolidation of the links between the campus and Washington has eroded the insulation between the vagaries of policies formulated by the government and the conduct of the higher learning. The alarms sounded by the more conservative members of the academic community about retaining the independence and autonomy of higher education against incursions from Washington became dulled as the volume of dollars flowing from the federal treasury to the colleges and universities continued to grow. But along with the benefits of federal programs have come costs, some relating to the growing dependence on the federal government for financial support, others to the increasing loss of institutional autonomy through federal provisions specifying, for example, the kinds of students eligible for federal support, or the requirement that states designate statewide planning commissions as condition for receiving federal money.[f]

The emergence of a politics of higher education has been defined largely by the efforts of the higher education community to adjust to the increasingly complicated interdependence of higher education and government. Specifically, the educators have sought to modify their organizations to play a more sustained and influential political role. At the same time, they have sought to accommodate their ideological ambivalence about an active political role with the political realities that have compelled higher education to become a visible contender in national interest politics.

Notes

1. Edward D. Eddy, Jr., *Colleges for Our Land and Time: The Land Grant Idea in American Education* (New York: Harper & Bros., 1956, 1957).

2. Quoted in Charles Dobbins, ed., *American Council on Education: Leadership and Chronology, 1918–1968* (Washington, D.C., 1968), pp. 1–2.

3. Ibid., p. 3.

4. Richard G. Axt, *The Federal Government and Financing Higher Education* (New York Columbia University Press, 1952), p. 74.

5. Ibid., p. 77–78.

6. Ibid., p. 81.

7. Hollis P. Allen, *The Federal Government and Education* (New York: McGraw Hill Book Company, 1950), p. 108.

8. Keith W. Olson, "A Historical Analysis of the G.I. Bill and Its Relationship to Higher Education," n.d. Available from the Educational Resources Information Center (ED 024 330).

9. James L. Sundquist, *Politics and Policy: The Eisenhower, Kennedy, and Johnson Years* (Washington, D.C.: The Brookings Institution, 1968), p. 179.

10. H. Douglas Price, "Race, Religion, and Rules Committee," in Allen F. Westin, ed., *The Uses of Power* (New York: Harcourt, Brace, 1962), pp. 1–71; and Sundquist, *Politics and Policy,* pp. 201–205.

---

[f] A provision in the 1972 amendments required that states designate planning commissions in order to receive certain funds under the law. Educators were concerned about the effects of powerful state planning agencies on their institutions. The fiscal 1974 budget, however, provided almost no functions for the state commissions to perform. *Chronicle of Higher Education,* March 19, 1973.

11. Thomas Wolanin and Lawrence Gladieux, "A Charter for Federal Policy Toward Post-secondary Education: The Education Amendments of 1972," *Journal of Law and Education* (forthcoming).

12. Thomas Wolanin and Lawrence Gladieux, "The Political Culture of a Policy Arena: Higher Education," in Matthew Holden and Dennis Dresang, eds., *The Yearbook of Politics and Public Policy,* Vol. I., (Sage, January 1975).

13. J. L. Penick, Jr., C. W. Pursell, Jr., M. B. Sherwood, and D. C. Swain, eds., *The Politics of American Science, 1939 to the Present* (Chicago: Rand McNally and Company, 1956), p. 52.

14. National Science Foundation, *Federal Support to Universities, Colleges, and Selected Non-Profit Institutions, Fiscal Year 1972* (Washington, D.C., 1974), p. viii.

15. Christian K. Arnold, "The Government and University Science: Purchase or Investment?" in Harold Orlans, ed., *Science Policy and the University* (Washington, D.C.: the Brookings Institute of 1968), pp. 89–100; and House Committee on Science and Astronautics Report, *National Program of Institutional Grants,* 91st Cong., 1st Sess., September 1968.

16. Christopher Jencks and David Riesman, *The Academic Revolution* (Garden City, N.Y.: Doubleday & Company, 1968).

17. Stephen Bailey and Edith Mosher, *ESEA: The Office of Education Administers a Law* (Syracuse: Syracuse University Press, 1968), pp. 17–18.

18. Harry Kursh, *The United States Office of Education: A Century of Service* (Philadelphia: Chilton Books, 1965), p. 21.

19. Bailey and Mosher, *ESEA,* p. 73.

20. Alvin W. Weinberg, "The New Estate," *Yale Scientific Magazine,* October 1963, p. 16. Emphasis added. Copyright © 1963, by Yale Scientific, reprinted by permission.

21. Lawrence K. Pettit, *The Politics of Federal Policymaking For Higher Education,* manuscript, ch. III, p. 13.

22. Ibid., p. 30.

2

The Structure of the Washington Higher Education Community

The rather abrupt increase in the number of offices, associations, and specialized organizations located in Washington during the mid- and late 1960s was a direct result of the rush of legislation passed during those years. To speak about the Washington higher education community is simply a short-hand term for the more than 50 such associations that make their home in the capital. The number and diversity of these associations lends credibility to the observation that "probably no other segment of American society has so many organizations and is yet so unorganized as higher education." [1]

Although the basis for cooperation within this community is voluntary and informal, there is an identifiable structure to the higher education community and a clear division of political labor. The need for cooperative efforts in such a setting has been clearly recognized. This awareness is reflected in a proposal submitted by the American Council on Education (ACE) to the W. K. Kellogg Foundation requesting funds to acquire a National Center for Higher Education on Washington's Dupont Circle. The request argued that

An intangible value fully as important as the services available is that the new Center will symbolize the unity of higher education. With the increasing involvement of the federal government in matters educational, it is more important than ever before for institutions of learning to be in effective communication with each other and to be well organized for the voluntary enterprise aspects of unified action. [2]

Not surprisingly, the six major institutional-membership associations, the Association of American Colleges (AAC), the American Association of Community and Junior Colleges (AACJC), the American Association of State Colleges and Universities (AASCU), the Association of American Universities (AAU), the American Council on Education (ACE), and the National Association of State Universities and Land-Grant Colleges (NASULGC), take part most regularly and on the widest range of political concerns of all the Washington-based higher education associations. Moreover, there is an extensive overlap in the membership of these six associations. For example, while the ACE, with over 1,300 members, is the largest of the associations, 80 per cent of its members hold membership in at least one of the other five organizations.[3] Organizations representing specialized constituencies within higher education, such as graduate schools, schools of law and medicine, and colleges with religious affiliations, are smaller, more specialized, and far less likely to get tangled up in any sustained way on issues that range beyond the interests of their rather specialized interests. Finally, the small offices representing state systems, individual schools, and consortia place their main emphasis on services to the membership, and not on political activities.

The Major Associations

American Council on Education (ACE)

The American Council on Education (ACE), higher education's so-called umbrella organization, was forged during World War I to help coordinate higher education's relations with the federal government. As higher education's most visible organization it has the most extensive membership and the most bountiful resources of any of the higher education associations. In March 1973 there were 194 national and regional associations and organizations, 1,379 colleges and universities embracing the full spectrum of American colleges and universities, and 59 affiliated institutions and organizations. Also included in this congregation are state departments of education, city and private school systems, secondary schools, libraries, and educational fraternities and societies.

Financially, the council has come a long way. In 1919 the first ACE director was delayed in assuming his full-time duties because the financial committee was having a hard time raising the $20,000 minimum budget. The 1972 working budget amounted to nearly $5 million. Major foundations like Ford, Carnegie, and Sloan have been exceedingly generous in their support of the Council. Early in 1968, for example, the W. K. Kellogg Foundation granted $2.5 million toward financing the National Center for Higher Education on Washington's Dupont Circle. The eight-story concrete and glass structure was completed early in 1970 and now houses some 39 associations and organizations associated with higher education. The ACE itself occupies the entire eighth floor with its staff of over 150 persons, and presides over the National Center in comfortable corporate fashion.

Like most large voluntary organizations the ACE is constrained in its pursuit of tangible political objectives by the diversity of its membership. ACE policy positions are deliberately general and reflect its efforts to avoid positions on programs of specific benefit to particular categories of institutions. Instead, it strives to arrive at policy positions that benefit as many members as possible. Statements have put major stress on equal educational opportunities for students, more effective and equitable patterns of federal financial support, and programs designed to assist the institutions in offsetting their operational costs.[4] Two themes have characterized ACE policy statements in recent years. One has been a tendency to state preferences in terms of adjustment, expansion, or administrative modification of existing programs with no substantial—not to say radical—departures from existing policies. A second theme has focused on the declining federal support for various programs and the frustrations and disruptions irregular and unpredictable federal support causes for colleges and universities. Late in 1969, for example, the ACE Federal Relations Commission issued a statement with a strong caution against shifting the burden of educational financing to the student, and reducing the national investment in higher education. The commission unequivocally rejected the idea that the burden of education funding can or should be shifted to future generations. In this context it argued that there had to be (1) a *sustained* commitment by the government to the financing of existing federally funded higher education programs; (2) a continuation of the existing combination of opportunity grants; (3) a substantial construction program supported by federal grants and loans; and (4) federal support for general institutional purposes.[5]

National Association of State Universities and Land-Grant Colleges (NASULGC)

The National Association of State Universities and Land-Grant Colleges (NASULGC) is composed of 130 colleges and universities: 71 land-grant institutions, 32 state universities, 1 urban university, and 26 major campuses of multicampus universities. The College of the Virgin Islands and the University of Guam were granted land-grant status in 1972. Two of the land-grant institutions, Cornell University and the Massachusetts Institute of Technology are privately controlled. The association is the product of a 1963 merger between the Association of State Universities and Land-Grant Colleges (founded in 1887); the National Association of State Universities (founded in 1895); and the State Universities Association (founded in 1918). These organizations are the nation's oldest associations of institutions of higher education.

Although the members of NASULGC make up less than five per cent of the more than 2,500 colleges and universities in the country, they enroll nearly 30 per cent of all students. In addition to enrolling a significant share of students in publicly-supported institutions, many of the land-grant and state institutions sustain national reputations on the basis of their graduate programs. The member schools award about 36 per cent of all four-year bachelor and first professional degrees, 42 per cent of all master's degrees, and 64 per cent of all doctorates.

The Washington office opened in 1947 and has remained small since that time; in early 1970 there were four full-time professional staff members and eight clerical workers. From the time the Washington office opened until his retirement in January 1970, Russell Thackery served as executive director. Thackery is a former newspaper reporter and journalism professor who had reported and taught in Kansas, Nebraska, Minnesota, and Tennessee before coming to Washington. In his tenure he became known as "the dean of Washington representatives," not only for his length of service, but also for his uniquely personal style in representing the interests of NASULGC members to government. He combined a reporter's instinct for unearthing news of policy and political importance to his members with a low-key style that kept him in continuous contact with administrators and policy makers. One former legislative official from the Department of Health, Education, and Welfare claimed that he

could not really say how or at what points he headed an organization where college presidents in all the states had both political savvy and contacts with their senators and congressmen. So when we called a meeting we were sure to invite Russ Thackery, Jack Morse [ACE's federal relations director] and several others, depending on how big we wanted to make the meeting. But, for example, we didn't feel we had to invite guys like ——— because he didn't contribute anything, and while he would bitch and moan that he had been left out, he really couldn't do much but cause a lot of aggravation.

The interest position of the land-grant schools is shaped in large part by the commitment to low-cost public education and the continued promotion of graduate study and research. These concerns have led to efforts to reassert some institutional leverage over the increasingly cumbersome and trying system of project grants and mission-oriented research. The major direction of NASULGC policy statements has been toward a program of institutional grants linked on a formula basis to the amount of federal support for scientific research in these institutions. Had such a formula been adopted in 1972 it would have worked to the distinct advantage of the large, research-oriented universities at the expense of the two- and four-year liberal arts institutions. With the passage of the Education Amendments of 1972, these schools have emphasized low tuition as first priority.[6]

The political resources of the land-grant schools are based on a long tradition of experience in state politics, the prestige of many of their presidents, and the personal skills of their Washington representatives. The basic resource available to the association according to one NASULGC officer was the university president.

The real clout rests with the college presidents, and not with the association proper. The problem, though, is the judicious use of these men to make the maximum use of their prestige without overexposing them. Perhaps I shouldn't express it this way, but we have good "internal discipline" among our member presidents, which we take care not to overuse. By internal discipline, I mean that generally they will respond when we contact them and bring their weight to bear in any way they could to influence legislation.

American Association of State Colleges and Universities (AASCU)

The American Association of State Colleges and Universities (AASCU) consists of 314 institutions located throughout the United States, the District of Columbia, Guam, and the Virgin Islands. Established in 1961, the AASCU represents the fastest growing degree-granting institutions in the country, the former normal or teacher's colleges, and state regional universities. The membership includes comprehensive state college and regional state universities that have developed from single-purpose teacher's colleges, newly established institutions, technological schools, and former municipal universities and junior colleges that have become state institutions. Enrollments have tripled over the past decade to a point where these schools account for about two million students, or about one of every four attending college. In addition, they award more than one-fourth of all the nation's bachelor's degrees and more than one-fifth of all master's degrees, and graduate about one-half of the country's potential teachers. In a capsule description of the essential character of the AASCU membership, one observer notes that:

Many of them until fairly recently have been relatively sleepy, single-purpose, teacher training colleges. Having acquired a taste for higher status and strong ambitions, they are at various stages of movement along a spectrum from their single-purpose origins as teachers colleges toward multi-purpose university status and prestige.[7]

The Washington office of the AASCU opened in 1962 and is now housed at the Dupont Circle National Center for Higher Education, just down the hall from the land-grant association. There are just five professional staff members and 16 clerical aids working out of the Washington office. Unlike the land-grant office, the AASCU performs a much more diverse range of services for its member institutions, first because there are so many more of them, and, more importantly, because they are generally unsophisticated about relations with Washington at a time when they are experiencing much more rapid change than the more mature members of the Washington higher education community.

In terms of political interests and representation, the AASCU staff has maintained a close working relationship with the land-grant association, to the extent that starting in 1967 the AASCU and the NASULGC held their annual meetings jointly and issued a joint statement outlining their political interests entitled "Recommendations for National Action Affecting Higher Education." [8] Although the interests of these two associations are identical at the national level, the members of these organizations compete with each other directly in the state legislatures and are in conflict over their respective roles in state higher education systems. There has, however, been much less disagreement among them nationally than locally.

Because it shares policy positions with the NASULGC, the AASCU has only recently mounted an independent effort at establishing its own legislative presence in Washington. By June 1973 the work of the AASCU Office of Federal Programs had shaken down and proved its value to its membership to the extent that the association leadership felt it could split off a new Office of Governmental Relations. This new office, headed by John Mallan, a former political operative with the community college association, was charged with more directly political (as opposed to service) responsibilities. These included the usual repertoire of congressional, executive, and state contacts, analysis of legislation, and tracking the implementation of federal programs.

Since the 1962 opening of the Washington office, the association has worked closely with the American Council. While it has occasionally offered supplementary testimony in support of legislation in which the ACE was not directly interested, it has generally testified in conjunction with representatives from the ACE, or has been represented by them to Congress.[9]

Aside from its newness in Washington, the AASCU has been hindered from developing a distinctive political presence because it lacks the resources available to associations like the NASULGC or an umbrella organization like the American Council. It is geared mainly to providing services for its members. Moreover, in terms of political leverage, the state colleges and most of the state universities lack the prestige and access built up by prominent educators and extensive research programs.

Association of American Colleges (AAC)

Where the NASULGC and the AASCU serve as the Washington spokesmen for the public-supported colleges and universities, the Association of American Colleges (AAC) represents the smaller, predominantly liberal arts colleges. The association was founded in 1915 to promote higher education in colleges of liberal arts and sciences. It now has a membership of approximately 780 schools of varying size, control, and religious affiliation; well over half are small, independent, or church-related. Its Washington office, one of the few not located in the National Center for Higher Education, opened in 1947 and is now staffed by some 20 professionals and clerical workers.

The policy stance of the AAC differs little from that of the other major associations. There are recommendations for a more equitable selective service, exhortations to equal educational opportunity to ameliorate poverty and racial discrimination, sufficient appropriations to sustain the programs of international education, and an enthusiastic endorsement of the continuation of the college housing program. The small, but in the past significant, differences in the AAC policy statement revolve around the explicit endorsement of equality of access to federal programs, which argues that it is "a fundamental principle of sound federal legislation and administrative policy that public institutions and private institutions, whether church-related or not, should be accorded equal access to all federal programs." [10] The number of church-related schools in the AAC makes this a point of particular interest to the association, which has provided active support to a court test of the legality of federal aid to denominationally tied colleges.[a]

The critical problems of financing the smaller liberal arts college took on an added urgency in the early part of 1971 when an association sponsored survey of some 500 schools indicated that the private colleges faced a rapidly deteriorating financial situation. It concluded that there was little hope for improvement unless significant aid was soon received from the federal government and other sources.[11] In every respect the AAC position on the financing of higher education has been almost identical to that of the other major associations. It has urged the federal government to expand its program of grants for academic facilities and to ease the matching requirements for such grants; establish a comprehensive student-aid plan that would emphasize grants rather than loans; and create a system of institutional grants for the support of general instruction in colleges and universities.

The major divide between the public and private institutions has been the advocacy of tax credits for personal expenditures in higher education by the AAC schools, a position heartily abhorred by the public institutions, and particularly by the land-grant schools. Tax credits had been viewed by private institutions as a device that would enable them to raise tuition levels, thus making the credits a form of indirect institutional support that would skirt the controversial church-state and public-private issues. In the

---

[a] The case, *Tilton* v. *Richardson*, was initiated by 15 Connecticut taxpayers challenging the constitutionality of direct federal grants to church-related colleges. A Supreme Court decision upheld the constitutionality of the law in the spring of 1971. See the *Chronicle of Higher Education*, July 5, 1971.

past several years, however, the AAC has backed off from tax credits as a means of financing education, to the point where the issue is just about dead.

Association of American Universities (AAU)

The Association of American Universities (AAU) is the representative arm of 48 of the nation's top research universities, including schools like Stanford, Yale, Harvard, the Universities of California, Minnesota, Indiana, Illinois, Virginia, and Iowa, as well as two Canadian universities, McGill and Toronto.[b] The aura of prestige that surrounds these universities is deceptive when viewed in terms of political representation, for it has been only within the past five or so years that the AAU schools have begun to act collectively in the promotion of their special interests.

For over half of its 70-year history, the AAU acted as a standardizing and accrediting organization; for much of its recent history, it has been a president's club.[12] University presidents met twice a year in closed sessions where deliberations were not made public and where explicit policy positions were rarely taken or publicized. It was not until 1962 that the AAU opened its Washington office, but even with this presence it remained content to let the American Council speak for the membership until creation of the Council on Federal Relations of 1969. (The evolution of the council is described in Chapter 5).

The interest position of the AAU member schools revolves around policies and programs of special interest to graduate education, particularly those tied to large-scale research support. For example, a 1968 policy statement recommended expanded student-aid programs and expanded federal support for colleges building construction. It argued that there existed a "special Federal interest in sustaining, extending, and strengthening graduate and professional education," and that this interest should be manifested in expanded graduate fellowships and traineeships, as well as increased cost-of-education supplements "more closely approximating the real educational costs to the institution."

It specifically called for "strong support of research in the universities

---

[b] The stature of the membership is reflected in a recent evaluation of reputation in 36 disciplines. In the ratings on faculty quality, for example, the University of California, Berkeley, placed 32 departments in the top category. Following in order, Harvard, 27; Stanford, 16; Chicago, 14; Yale, 13; M.I.T., 12; Michigan, 12; Princeton, 12; California Institute of Technology, 11; Wisconsin, 9; Illinois, 6; Columbia, 5. See Kenneth D. Roose and Charles J. Andersen, *A Rating of Graduate Programs* (Washington, D.C.: American Council on Education, 1970).

and provision for its continuing development" where federal funds would pay the full costs of federally sponsored research. Moreover, if colleges and universities were to play an effective problem-solving role in urban affairs or environmental pollution, then new funding would have to be provided. Finally, the statement endorsed, with some reservations, the institution of broadly based institutional support for colleges and universities as a necessary supplement to their existing sources of support. The major reservation turned on the fear that any formula for such an institutional grants program would not recognize "the levels and types of instruction and their widely varying costs," or in other words, that it costs more to educate a doctoral candidate than a student pursuing either a bachelor's or a master's degree.[13]

Although the resources for promoting these interests are in many respects like those of the other major associations, they differ markedly in both amount and caliber. As noted above, the AAU presidents have until very recently been able to exploit the aura of their institutional prestige, and the respect accorded them as individuals, to insure at least the opportunity for a patient hearing. They are also well-connected to those versatile persons who circulate in and out of the major corporations, foundations, universities, and government—those who are aware and sensitive to the special needs and problems of higher education, but more importantly, who are in positions to take action. Because these universities sustain extensive research programs, there are also continuous contacts between campus and the Washington officials in the principal granting agencies like NSF and NIH.

The AAU federal relations effort promises to be a firm asset, as it was designed to be, in representing the elite universities in Washington. The staff consists of three professionals, has substantial autonomy, and is not burdened with peripheral services like grant applications or newsletter writing. Legislative targets have been carefully selected and alliances and coalitions negotiated, for example with the Association of American Medical Colleges and the American Medical Association on increased support to medical education. Such selective activity is further made possible by the willingness to utilize the information and additional resources of other associations, particularly the American Council's federal relations office.

*American Association of Community and
Junior Colleges (AACJC)*

The remaining major higher education association in Washington is the American Association of Community and Junior Colleges (AACJC). It was established in 1920 to represent the interests, to stimulate the professional development, and to promote the sound growth of American two-year colleges. It now speaks for some 875 member institutions. The association offices moved to the capital in 1939, and in 1971 employed nearly 30 professional staff members and a total office force of about 60, making it second only to the ACE in the size and diversity of its activities.

Along with the four-year state colleges, the two-year junior colleges comprise the most rapidly expanding segment of American higher education. In 1968, for example, there were some 802 such schools; in 1970 there were 891—237 private and 654 public. More than 90 per cent of the students attending the two-year institutions are enrolled in publicly supported schools.

The interest position of the junior colleges is shaped in large part by the diversity of its clientele and its particular emphasis upon providing a wide range of educational opportunity, including vocational and occupational training. Thus the AACJC has worked to participate in programs for nurse training, education in the allied health professions, and various vocational educational legislation—programs that the other major associations have little interest in pursuing. One consequence of moving into these areas has been to generate conflicts outside the normal boundaries of the Washington higher education community. These cut across a whole new spectrum of interests such as those controlling accreditation for nurse's training and groups with stakes in vocational education. In addition, the AACJC shares the concerns of the other major associations for the kinds of general educational measures designed to aid students and support construction costs.

In spite of a general lack of institutional or presidential prestige, or extensive access to the executive branch, the junior colleges do possess some fundamental political resources, often in sufficient abundance that they are viewed with some degree of envy and no small amount of discomfort by their colleagues. The basic resource of the AACJC and its members is the fact that there is at least one community college in nearly every congressional district in the country. This situation might be little more than a geographical curiosity were it not for the fact that the AACJC federal relations operation has an extremely effective communication system that can quickly mobilize support from the states.

Equally important, the loyalty and enthusiasm of the AACJC itself have helped move the two-year colleges from step-child status in the Washington community to that of an assertive, autonomous organization. A new sense of self-assurance, a strong dose of egalitarian individualism, plus a large and frequently resourceful staff have created a situation where the community colleges have gained the capacity to pursue their own interests independently of the other associations.

The Special-Interest Associations

The special-interest or satellite associations are those that represent a fairly specialized constituency within the context of the more comprehensive associations. Except on issues of specific interest to their members, they are generally willing to let the major associations speak for them. They tend to cluster in two main orbits, one of which is more frequently connected to the research, graduate, and professional programs characteristic of the NASULGC and AAU schools; the second is linked more closely to the AAC liberal arts colleges, and the teacher education programs that historically have been the province of the AASCU colleges.

Included in the first orbit are those schools whose basic ties are with the NASULGC and the AAU, primarily the Council of Graduate Schools in the United States, the Association of American Medical Colleges, the Association of American Law Schools, the National Association of College and University Business Officers, and the National Council of University Research Administrators. These organizations deal basically with the kinds of interests inherent in these special clienteles, not with the institutions as a whole. Consequently they are far more likely to take their cues from and have far more frequent contacts with their associated professional groups (the American Bar Association, the American Medical Association, and so forth) than the major higher education associations. While the associations do meet on issues of common concern such as tax policy or copyright law, there is far less contact around broader, more substantive policy questions.

These kinds of satellite organizations are clearly based on large-scale research interests, specialized professional education, and patterns of alliances that draw heavily from interests outside the regular higher education community. They stand in sharp contrast to the associations whose primary focal point is the Association of American Colleges. These organizations represent special kinds of institutions, particularly colleges with religious affiliations, and those colleges of marginal status and financial condition.[c]

Ostensibly the associations linked closely to the AAC have a marked religious orientation; yet on close examination, the question of religious affiliation has subsided to a point where these colleges view most of their

---

[c] The one institutionally based association that overlaps extensively in both these groups is the American Association of Colleges of Teacher Education (AACTE), which represents 852 institutions that have teacher education programs. Until 1969 the AACTE shied away from establishing a governmental relations program because it felt that more often than not it would be in competition with other associations to which its members belonged. In 1969, however, the association set up its own federal relations program, and in doing so, acknowledged the increased importance of the federal government in programs relating to teacher education.

troubles as those of private colleges, not religious schools. The 350 colleges and universities affiliated with the Roman Catholic Church in the United States are represented by the executive secretary (and one secretary) of the College and University Department of the National Catholic Educational Association (NCEA).[14] Because membership in the department overlaps extensively with the memberships of the AAC and the American Association of Colleges of Teacher Education (AATCE), the Washington Office has had little need to speak for its membership in the capital. Since Catholic schools are in fact private schools, their interests are identical to those of other private and church-related colleges—financial aid for students and a basic concern for liberal arts education. Consequently the NCEA's legislative interests are assumed by the AAC, and where appropriate, through the other major associations.

The diminishing strength of religious identity is reflected in the rather unique spectacle of organizational life, the voluntary dismantling of an ongoing organization. The Council of Protestant Colleges and Universities (CPCU) was organized in 1958 and first convened in 1959 to represent Protestant colleges and universities in Washington and to further the role of the church-related college in American higher education. By 1966 the CPCU membership included more than 230 Protestant institutions, many of which were members of the AAC. During 1970, 55 institutions had either withdrawn from the council or failed to pay their dues. In addition to declining membership and income in recent years, many council members felt that the need for an organization representing only Protestant institutions had decreased, and that the problems of their institutions were inseparable from those of other private institutions.

The third association linked to the AAC is the Council for the Advancement of Small Colleges (CASC). Founded in 1956, the CASC claims that it is the only national education association that focuses its attention solely on the problems of the small, private, independent four-year college of liberal arts. The primary concern of CASC has been to provide its 140 members with a collective means of achieving regional accreditation more quickly and effectively than might be possible through independent efforts. Once accreditation has been attained, CASC acts as a service and consultative organization that assists member colleges in efforts to expand enrollments; raise academic standards; encourage academic experimentation and innovation; strengthen financial resource; and build liaison with other educational associations and federal government departments and agencies.

The AAC satellite organizations, the dissolved CPCU, the CASC, and the College and University Department of the NCEA, have clearly defined institutional constituencies, none of which is particularly potent in the realm of higher education politics and each of which prefers to look to more comprehensive associations on political matters. They are limited in terms of style, time, funds, and contacts. Moreover, they are inhibited by the value concerns of church-related schools and their uncertain status in terms of receiving federal funds.[d] In spite of the deficiency in resources for pursuing governmental relations, it is for these small private liberal arts colleges that continued contact with political and administrative decision makers is extremely critical. For many of these schools it is a matter of survival.

State Offices, Small Associations, and Private Grantsmen

Until about 1963, the major associations provided the locus for the Washington higher education community. Following the deluge of higher education bills passed during the Kennedy and Johnson administrations there emerged a new and distinctive pattern of institutional representation in the capital, the individual representative of a single institution or group of institutions. The four essential parts to this emerging pattern are offices representing state systems, small associations of fairly homogeneous institutions, individual colleges and universities, and schools enlisting the services of private entrepreneurs.[15]

State Systems

The model state system office has been that of the State University of New York (SUNY). It opened in 1965 in the wake of the Kennedy and Johnson higher education legislation as a branch of the chancellor's office and was commissioned to perform two major tasks. First, it was to promote the new and relatively unknown state system to those in Washington. More importantly, it was to help assure that SUNY received its full share of federal funds for education.

The overall objectives of the Washington office were expressed with candor in the first annual report: "Helping SUNY get federal funds continues to be the major objective of the Washington office. In this role, the office is middleman, performing essentially a facilitative service between the Federal Government—the source of funds and the producer of vast amounts of information—and SUNY, potentially a huge consumer of Federal funds and information. In the long run, therefore, information processing becomes a key to the success of the Washington office opera-

---

[d] Both the president of the CPCU and the executive secretary of the College and University Department of NCEA were active in a committee headed by Willis M. Tate, president of Southern Methodist University, that was formed to defray their legal costs in the *Tilton* v. *Richardson* case.

tion." Offices representing South Dakota's public colleges, the University of California, the California State Colleges, and the University of Texas performed similar services for their constituents starting in the late 1960s and into the 1970s.

Small Associations

The small associations are those with a limited and fairly homogeneous membership, and whose primary objectives—like those of the other offices discussed in this chapter—involve better access to information about federal policies and government funds for higher education. They fall into three main groups: associations of schools with religious affiliations, predominantly black colleges, and cooperative arrangements of similar kinds of colleges.

There are two main associations of schools based on religious affiliation, the Association of Jesuit Colleges and Universities and the Lutheran Council. The Jesuit-sponsored colleges and universities comprise one of the most important segments of Catholic higher education in the country. Although they represent less than 10 per cent of all these schools, they enroll about one-third of all students in Catholic colleges and universities. The association (until 1971 the Jesuit Education Association) moved its headquarters from Detroit to Washington in 1962 to be closer to the federal action. The colleges affiliated with the Lutheran church are represented through the Division of Education Services for the Lutheran Council in the United States. In many respects it is far less structured but has a broader constituency than its Jesuit counterpart.

In small offices like these, such variables as personal capabilities and preferences, organizational support, and political perceptions assume inflated importance in contrast to larger offices that can sustain specialized staffs and that have carved out some relatively explicit political objectives and commissioned their staffs to carry them out.

While the Jesuit and Lutheran associations are linked by common religious affiliations, the approximately 114 predominantly black colleges and universities are tied by racial identification and geographic location. In 1969 these schools, located mostly in the South-Atlantic region, enrolled nearly 300,000 students, about one-third of whom attended the 34 public Negro colleges.[e] Until the formation of the College Service Bureau in 1969

---

[e] Early in 1970 some 111 public and private black colleges formed the National Association for Equal Opportunity in Higher Education. The basic objective of the new association was to bring the views of these college presidents to bear on national educational policy and to try to influence decisions in both public and private circles

the colleges were represented in Washington through the land-grant and state college associations. The NASULGC maintains an Office for the Advancement of Public Negro Colleges in Atlanta, Georgia, which works with these schools to help them increase their share of private voluntary support.

The College Service Bureau opened its Washington office in the fall of 1969 to establish a federal relations effort for the small colleges. The fact that the office is supported by the United Negro College Fund and the Phelp-Stokes Fund's Cooperative College Development Program makes it quite clear that the bureau's clientele will come primarily from black colleges and universities.

The last important kind of small association is that based on voluntary cooperation, or a consortium arrangement. In 1970 there were only two such offices representing federations of colleges, the Associated Colleges of the Midwest (ACM) and the East Central College Consortium. The ACM is a federation of 10 midwestern liberal arts colleges sharing an office in Chicago and Washington.[f]

The Washington office opened in 1966 under the direction of Ida Wallace, a former *Newsweek* reporter and staff member of Bell Educational Associates, an educational consulting firm. Like the other small associations, the role played by the two-man ACM Washington office is limited by its size and resources, and contingent largely on the personal skills and inclinations of Mrs. Wallace. The East Central College Consortium, made up of a similar coalition of seven small liberal arts colleges, established a Washington office in September 1968.[g]

The potential for personal contact and familiarity with the administration, staff, and faculty of the member schools is a strong impetus for the maintenance of a Washington office among the smaller colleges. There is a pervasive feeling that the major associations, even with their federal relations programs, are simply unable to keep abreast of the needs and special characteristics of the various members. What these offices lack in

---

regarding the financing of higher education. One motivation for creating yet another organization was the feeling that in the past, black colleges and universities had little to say about higher education policy; hence programs and policies that had been developed ostensibly to aid Negro and other colleges operating at competitive disadvantage did not effectively benefit such colleges. Moreover, these schools had little to say about programs and policies directed toward equalizing educational opportunity for the so-called disadvantaged student. As of early 1971, the NAEOHE had not established a permanent Washington office. Vivian W. Henderson, "Unique Problems of Black Colleges," *Liberal Education* LVI (October 1970): 373–83.

[f] The ACM member colleges are Beloit, Carleton, Coe, Cornell, Grinnell, Knox, Lawrence, Monmouth, Ripon, and St. Olaf.

[g] The ECCC member colleges are Bethany, Heidelberg, Hiram, Marietta, Mount Union, Muskingum, and Westminster.

funding or staff, they make up for in direct, highly personalized kind of liaison established between Washington and the membership.

Representatives for Individual Schools

The ultimate form of representation is to have your own man in Washington. Such a representative can come in a variety of forms. Those from schools like Rutgers, Wisconsin, Harvard, and Indiana do not maintain offices in the capital, but fly in, often for several days at a time, to transact university business. Then they return to their campuses where they are frequently vice-presidents for research and advanced studies, educational development, or research administration. This form of representation hinges largely on institutional prestige, personal contacts, and sufficient proximity to Washington to make such shuttle flights personally and financially feasible.

Washington-based representatives for individual schools are frequently alumni, members of local law firms, or, in a few instances, professional lobbyists. Schools enlisting alumni or alumnae range from Sweetbriar, a small Virginia girls' school of about 800 students, to Ohio State University, a school enrolling some 46,000 students. Like most of the other representatives, they are commissioned to help review government programs, provide information to the faculty, and assist in any way possible—including writing and submitting proposals. The major difference is that the task is restricted to a single school, the resources are even more meager than the offices of the small associations, and political action is limited to contacts with representatives and senators from the state, and then only in very special instances.

In contrast to these part-time roles, the University of Houston and the University of Oklahoma have recently set up offices in the National Center for Higher Education, the Dupont Circle home of the Washington higher education establishment. Both offices opened in 1970, and both resulted in part from the feeling that the major associations simply did not have the staff, resources, facilities, or inclination to pursue the interests of a single school, even though substantial portions of the University budgets come from the federal government.

Private Entrepreneurs

American enterprise has shown an uncanny sense of where to seek new profits. The harvest of higher education legislation after 1963 provided a potential new area of entrepreneurial activity and gave rise to the so-called middleman in the grants and contracts aspect of federal relations. There were three main kinds of private entrepreneurs operating in Washington during the 1960s: fund-raising public relations firms that simply expanded their operations, former government personnel who formed their own consulting firms, and former educators who moved into the profit-making side of higher education.[16] With few exceptions, all were designed to be profit-making operations, and with equally few exceptions, most were driven out of business with federal spending cutbacks and the creation of federal relations operations within the major associations.

For the most part, the private entrepreneurs limited their roles to that of middlemen, and while an occasional brochure would advertise congressional liaison as one function, their basic services involved guiding clients to appropriate sources of funds, helping formulate research and development ideas, following through on accepted proposals, and analyzing rejected proposals for resubmission. Some of the more blatantly commercial firms advertised their availability for auditing, editing, and guiding them "through the Washington labyrinth" while maintaining "close, cordial relations with the appropriate government officials."

Although several of these firms have continued to represent colleges and universities in Washington, many have fallen victim to federal spending cutbacks and questions about the legitimacy of their role in higher education. Survival for such firms seemed to be largely a function of their own reputations and ability to diversify their consulting operations so that their services and clientele extended beyond colleges and universities. With the exception of a very few firms like Bell Educational Services, most such operations were never able to overcome the skepticism and mistrust college administrators and government officials had toward private entrepreneurs. Businessmen tended to bring their own values, oriented far more explicitly toward efficient operations and profit-making, than to education, thus creating serious communications difficulties between the entrepreneurs and educators. Moreover, such firms tended to oversell the efficacy of their contacts with the various federal agencies. While most agency spokesmen readily conceded the valuable role such firms could play as conduits for information, they were virtually unanimous in their contention that they would prefer to deal with the individuals concerned with research proposals rather than middlemen purporting to speak for such applicants.[17]

The structure of representation in Washington then, is one with a core of higher education associations, each with a substantial yet identifiable institutional constituency, distinctive interests, and an individual tone and posture toward political action. The five major associations—AAC, AAU, AASCU, AACJC and NASULGC—as well as the American Council, are in frequent contact with one another, and are regularly alert to the policy and political stakes of higher education. They have had the experience, the resources, and the largest numbers of constituents to provide a broad basis for political activity. To say that they represent the core of the higher education establishment is not an ideological location, but simply an indication that they provide the central framework within which the Washington representatives conduct their day-to-day business.

At the periphery of these major associations are the two distinctive groups of satellite associations, those based in graduate professional education, and those based in the small, private liberal arts colleges. The graduate-professional schools work not only through the major education associations, but have allies in regular professional groups like the American Bar Association and the American Medical Association. In sharp contrast, the small college associations like CASC, CPCU, and NCEA lack such external support and resources and hence must turn regularly to the major associations for political representation. Similarly, the limited resources and specialized services provided by the offices of the state systems, small associations, and private entrepreneurs compel these representatives to remain at the fringes of the policy-making community.

Notes

1. Homer D. Babbidge and Robert M. Rosenzweig, *The Federal Interest in Higher Education* (New York: McGraw-Hill Book Company, Inc., 1962), p. 92.

2. *National Center for Higher Education.* A brochure published by the American College Public Relations Association, Summer 1972.

3. Roger W. Heyns, "The National Educational Establishment: Its Impact on Federal Programs and Institutional Policies," *Liberal Education,* May 1973, p. 152.

4. See, for example, "The Federal Investment in Higher Education: the Need for Sustained Commitment" (American Council on Education: Washington, D.C., 1967); "Federal Programs for Higher Education: Needed Next Steps" (American Council on Higher Education: Washington, D.C., 1969); and "An Outline for Federal Action," *Educational Record,* Winter 1971, pp. 1–9. This last statement places a clear emphasis on the need for federal funds to support institutional operating costs.

5. American Council on Education Press Release, February 10, 1970.

6. See, for example, Recommendations for National Action Affecting Higher Education. A Joint Statement. American Association of State Colleges and Universities and National Association of State Universities and Land-Grant Colleges, January 1974.

7. E. Alden Dunham, *Colleges of the Forgotten Americans: A Profile of State Colleges and Regional Universities* (New York: McGraw-Hill Book Company, 1969), p. xii.

8. AASCU and NASULGC, Recommendations.

9. Harland G. Bloland, *Higher Education Associations in a Decentralized Education System* (Center for Research and Development in Higher Education, University of California, Berkeley, 1969).

10. "Statement of Policy on Federal Relations with Higher Education," *Liberal Education,* March 1969, p. 165; entire statement, pp. 163–67.

11. William Jellema, "The Red and the Black," Special Preliminary Report on the Financial Status, Present and Projected, of Private Institutions of Higher Learning, n.d., released 1971.

12. William K. Selden, "The AAU—Higher Education's Enigma," *Saturday Review,* March 19, 1966, pp. 76–78, sketches the history of the AAU.

13. Association of American Universities, *The Federal Financing of Higher Education* (April 1968).

14. Andrew M. Greeley, *From Backwater to Mainstream: A Profile of Catholic Higher Education* (New York: McGraw-Hill Book Company, 1969).

15. Several articles have commented on the Washington representative for higher education. See Frank Clifford, "Washington Outpost: More Schools Find Use for a Man in the Capital," *Science* 159 (March 22, 1968): 1334–40; Mark Levy, "The University Lobbyists," *The Reporter,* June 30, 1966; and Ed Willingham, "Washington Pressures/Nation's Colleges, Universities Set up Office to Deal with Government," *National Journal,* April 14, 1971, pp. 844–52.

16. Lauriston R. King, "Higher Education's Vanishing Grantsmen," *Change Magazine,* May 1972.

17. Stephen Strickland, "Research Grants and Middlemen," in Stephen Strickland, ed., *Sponsored Research in American Universities and Colleges* (Washington, D.C.: American Council on Education, 1968), pp. 185–95.

3

The Washington Representatives: Who They Are and What They do

The political resources of the Washington offices are limited in money, control over the popular media, and capacity to influence electoral outcomes. Instead, they must rely on the prestige of higher education, the good will accorded member institutions and their presidents, and the personal skills and perseverance of the professionals who staff their associations. In most respects the personal characteristics and routine activities of the education representatives are not significantly different from those in other Washington corporate, religious, citizen or trade association offices. Their main labors revolve around getting the funds and prerogatives already promised by the federal government, and protecting these while trying to get more of them. Although these activities are not always so neatly defined, getting what is available is primarily the role of the grantsman, while protecting and promoting the interests of higher education is the job of the association lobbyist.

Personal Characteristics

The higher education representatives are not much different from representatives in other interest areas.[a] One earlier study of Washington lobbyists by Lester Milbrath found that they were nearly all from the upper middle class, had very high incomes and educations compared to the general population, and were mostly middle-aged, white, male, and Protestant.[1] Data on the higher education representatives provided by usable questionnaire returns from 48 of 59 representatives interviewed in 1969 and 1970 revealed few important distinctions from the Milbrath sample.

---

[a] There is only the faintest hint that descriptive biographical data can do any more than imply that there are connections between personal characteristics and political behavior in a small, elite group. See, for example, Lewis J. Edinger and Donald D. Searing, "Social Background in Elite Analysis: A Methodological Inquiry," *American Political Science Review* LXI (June 1967): 428–45. Such data can, however, furnish comparable information to other groups of political actors and thus provide a basis for describing a particular kind of skill group or nascent political role. In addition, such data can provide baselines against which to measure change without raising the causal dilemmas bound up in efforts to link demographic characteristics to political attitudes and behavior.

They also tended to be middle-aged, white, and Protestant, with extremely high educational attainment. The average age of the higher education representative was 52 years; 90 per cent were men; and 44 per cent identified themselves as Protestants (Table 3–1). Women clearly lack the status of their male counterparts in the higher education establishment. No woman held a policy or executive position in either the major or the special interest associations. Only two of the six held important full-time positions in the membership organizations, one as director of a consortium, the other as director of a state office. One was a private entrepreneur who headed her own firm; another represented several small Virginia colleges on a part-time basis; and one worked as a part-time director of a consortium office. There was an even more marked absence of Negro representatives.

Table 3–1

Sex, Age, Religious, and Educational Characteristics of Higher Education Representatives

Characteristics	Per Cent	Number
Sex		
Male	90	55
Female	10	6
Total	100	61
Age		
25–39	20	9
40–49	36	16
50–59	22	10
60–69	18	8
No answer	4	2
Total	100	45
Religion		
Protestant	44	21
Catholic	10	5
Jewish	4	2
Other	4	2
None	8	4
No answer	29	14
Total	99	48
Education		
Some high school	—	—
Finished high school	—	—
Some college	—	—
Finished college (B.A.)	21	10
Graduate or professional training (M.A.)	25	12
Professional degree (law)	21	10
Ph.D. or equivalent	33	16
No answer	—	—
Total	100	48

There were no blacks in the sample of Washington lobbyists, and only one in the higher education group. No black held an executive position in the major or satellite associations. The one black in the sample headed up the small office of a new association representing predominantly Negro colleges.

One predictable characteristic of the higher education representatives is their high educational attainment. In March 1970, 11 per cent of the population 25 years old and over had completed four or more years of college.[2] All the education representatives had completed at least four years of college; 46 per cent had received graduate or professional degrees; and a full 33 per cent had obtained the Ph.D.[b] It is hardly surprising that Ph.D. holders should be so disproportionately represented in a community where the degree is an occupational necessity and a mark of academic respectability. Paradoxically, it is not a credential that brings substantial political currency with it.

In terms of partisan identification, significantly more higher education representatives (47 per cent) declare themselves Democratic identifiers than Milbrath's sample of lobbyists (34 per cent), but the partisan preferences actually seem to have little impact on the work of either group (Table 3–2). Interviews with the education representatives confirm Mil-

Table 3–2

Party Identification of Higher Education Representatives and Washington Lobbyists

Party Identification	Higher Education Representatives		Washington Lobbyists[a]	
	%	Number	%	Number
Strong Democrat	37	19	15	17
Weak Democrat	10	5	19	22
Independent	25	13	23	26
Weak Republican	10	5	16	18
Strong Republican	4	2	13	15
Presidential Republican	7	4	3	3
No answer	7	4	11	13
Total	100	52	100	114

[a] Adapted from Lester W. Milbrath, *The Washington Lobbyists*, (Chicago: Rand McNally & Co., 1963), p. 77.

---

[b] Both the Washington lobbyists and the education representatives had far more formal education than the general population, and with it, enhanced income and social status. For example, slightly more than three-quarters of the lobbyists received at least a bachelor's degree, and 53 per cent received graduate or professional diplomas. Lester W. Milbrath, *The Washington Lobbyists,* (Chicago: Rand McNally & Co., 1963), p. 69.

brath's conclusion that the party with which an individual identifies appears to be relatively unimportant in lobbying. The disproportionately high 37 per cent of representatives expressing a strong Democratic identification reflects the generally more liberal stance of the academic community as well as the typically higher levels of awareness about politics and political issues than the general population. In addition, education as an abstract idea holds down one corner of the health and welfare triumvirate around which political battles have most frequently divided along liberal-conservative lines. In such fights the Democrats have traditionally and ideologically been more sympathetic to a broader, more generous distribution of educational values than their Republican counterparts.

Characteristics like age, sex, religious preference, educational background and party affiliation do little more than indicate that the higher education representatives do not comprise a unique group among other Washington representatives. With the exception of educational attainment and a tendency to be a bit younger and more Democratic than the Milbrath sample, the differences between the two groups are hardly impressive.

The job experience of the representatives before joining the higher education community has tended to be in areas that nurture politically related skills, including staff positions in the legislative and executive branches, communications-related activities in public relations and journalism, and law. Persons with experience in the executive branch have not been extensively recruited by higher education; only eight (17 per cent) of the representatives have held positions in this part of the government. There are several reasons for the limited recruitment from the executive offices and agencies. Basically, in spite of the upsurge of higher education legislation in the 1960s, the laws and administrative regulations for implementing these policies are still miniscule compared to the accumulated body of regulations, laws, and details affecting labor, business, or agriculture. Consequently, there is not an extensive reservoir of men who have administered these programs and who can be particularly knowledgeable and valuable to an organization affected by these programs and regulations. Moreover, the interests of higher education in the executive branch, aside from gaining the ear of the president and his staff, is pretty much limited to the Office of Education and other granting agencies like the National Science Foundation, the National Institutes of Health, or the Department of Defense. The higher education community has generally held the Office of Education in such low esteem (with the exception of a few individuals) that it has not been viewed as a source of skilled manpower for higher education's Washington political operation.

Eight representatives (17 per cent) also had had congressional experience, usually as administrative or legislative assistants. Business and law also provided experience for the representatives, but there were far fewer lawyers among the representatives than usually found working as lobbyists. Seven (15 per cent) of the representatives reported prior experience in business, and six (13 per cent) in law firms. Interestingly, nine (19 per cent) of the education representatives had written for newspapers or magazines. If experience in public relations firms is added to this figure, 12 (25 per cent) of those in the Washington higher education community have done at least some research and writing for popular consumption. Skills and perspectives acquired from journalism and public relations seem especially appropriate for positions that demand continuous exchange and communication both within the Washington political and administrative arenas and outside to clients and members around the country.

Occupational background may have nurtured skills and capabilities of particular value to Washington representatives but in the case of both lobbyists and representatives, very few had any on-the-job training in government. What is striking about the sample of formally registered Washington lobbyists is that 69 per cent of them had no experience on the Hill prior to their lobbying activities.[3] Ostensibly, the higher education representatives had far more experience in this respect, for only 52 per cent claimed no experience in the federal government. If special consultants and other advisory positions are excluded though, the total with no more than brief experience in government climbs to 66 per cent (Table 3–3).

When over two-thirds of the representatives and lobbyists have had no experience in the government they seek to influence, there is at least room to question whether these men have acquired the fine knowledge of the interstices of the policy process to become irresistible forces in Washington politics. To be sure, there are lobbyists and representatives who are knowledgeable and who have cultivated strategic contacts, but these men are

Table 3–3

Prior Positions in the Federal Government Held by Higher Education Representatives

Position in	Per Cent	Number
Department of Health, Education, and Welfare	2	1
Office of Education	2	1
Congressional committee staff	6	3
Congressional administrative or legislative staff	10	5
Executive staff	13	6
Special consulting	8	4
Other	6	3
None	52	25
Total	99	48

more likely to be full-time political operatives whose every working moment is spent interpreting the changing policy situations and acting on them for their clients. When interests are represented by men with only a routine understanding of the policy or administrative process, and who are pressed by a host of other service demands from their clients, then it seems unlikely that the interests they represent will come on as high-powered juggernauts relentlessly pressing their demands on decision makers.

Occupational experience and recruitment information also suggest that higher education is moving away from enlisting those with experience exclusively in the colleges and universities to those with experience in government and politics. This shift in recruitment is one concrete indication of higher education's development as a self-conscious interest group. No longer are the status and prestige criteria dominant within higher education sufficient as criteria for the selection of individuals mainly responsible for political activities. For example, of those the two representatives holding positions in the Washington higher education community for more than six years, only 29 per cent had held a position in the federal government; of those working from three to six years in Washington (which correspond to the years when much of the higher education legislation was passed), 52 per cent had had federal government experience. Nor does there appear to be any serious reversal of this tendency, for of those in positions for less than two years, 50 per cent have worked in the government (Table 3–4). Three representatives recruited after these data were collected had government experience, one as an administrative assistant on the Hill, another as an official in the Public Health Service, and the third in the Office of Education.

There appears to be an increasing willingness by higher education policy makers within colleges, universities, and governing boards of the

Table 3–4

Higher Education Representatives with Prior Federal Government Experience and Length of Time in Current Position

Length of Time in Washington Higher Education Position	Prior Position in Federal Government[a]	
	Per Cent	Number
Less than 2 years (N = 9)	50	18
3 to 6 years (N = 12)	52	23
Over 6 years (N = 2)	29	7

[a] Excludes representatives with no experience in federal government.

Table 3–5

Higher Education Representatives with Prior Position in Higher Education and Length of Time in Current Position

Length of Time in Washington Higher Education Position	Prior Position in Higher Education	
	Per Cent	Number
Less than 2 years (N = 12)	67	18
3 to 6 years (N = 19)	100	19
Over 6 years (N = 7)	100	7

associations to recruit persons who have not necessarily had teaching or administrative experience, but who have some experience and familiarity with the ways of Washington political life (Table 3–5).

Although two-thirds of the newcomers to the higher education community still come from positions in higher education, there is a marked decline in the tendency to recruit representatives directly from the colleges and universities. Those in Washington with more than three years all held positions in higher education; but of the most recent members of the community, those with less than two years' tenure in Washington, only 67 per cent came from academic or administrative positions. Certainly such experience is not a prerequisite for an effective representative, but it does enhance a representative's skills, knowledge, and access if he has had some prior operating experience navigating his way through the Congress and the agencies.

The Job of the Washington Representative

The preceding discussion has repeatedly talked about the Washington representative, his personal characteristics, and the structural setting within which he moves. No attention, however, has been paid to the nature of representation itself. The key element in the representative's role involves sensitivity and awareness of a client's interests, substantial amounts of autonomy for both parties in the relationship, and the submergence of conflict wherever feasible. In a nonlegislative setting, the representative is dependent upon the maintenance and predictability of these conditions to perform the three essential parts of his role: (1) serving the needs and immediate demands of his constituents; (2) acting as the diplomatic agent of his constituents in Washington; and (3) trying to influence policy formation and administration.

The common endeavor that links these three functions is the communication of information and political intelligence. Lewis Dexter, describing the way in which interests are represented in Washington, contends that there is no reason for most Washington representatives to spend the bulk of their time on legislative lobbying because they deal most fundamentally in information. He explains that "the Washington representative must select, process, and handle information so that it becomes 'intelligence,' in the sense in which the word is used in military planning. For, in one way or another, clients and employers are concerned with actions or contemplated actions; and information is only useful to them if it affects plans for action." [4] The critical point is that *"the effective Washington representative provides influence for his client by acquiring and translating relevant information."* [5] It is too much to claim that information is tantamount to influence, but information does facilitate the exploitation of resources available from government and greatly enhances the *potential* for taking political action aimed at exerting influence in the policy process.

Services for the Membership

In a word, the basic service the higher education representatives provide for members is aid in grantsmanship, the increasingly organized and systematic effort to reap the harvest of federal policies directed toward higher education. The bulk of this work takes place in the offices of the small associations and state and individual university offices, although both the AASCU and the AAC have attempted to provide these services in the past few years. Most of the work in this service area is fairly mundane and differs little from the work done by Washington representatives in other interest areas.[c] Specifically, they funnel information back to the campuses about guidelines, deadlines, and eligibility for grants and programs; assist in drafting and reviewing proposals prior to submission; and watch them as they move through the agency reviewing process. When possible they find out from agency reviewers how a rejected proposal might

---

[c] For example, business representatives not only try to market their company's products, but seek out research and development contracts, thus serving as a bridge between company and government. From his continuing contacts with government agencies the representative is able to spot the need for, and call upon, various company experts or specialists. His role is much like that of the higher education representative who tries to make the agencies aware of the special capabilities of his schools and faculty. In the case of both business and higher education representatives, "his success depends in part on his keeping abreast of what the government wants or may want in the future and in part on his intimate knowledge of his company's capabilities and personnel. His role is simultaneously that of salesman, technician, and business ambassador." Paul W. Cherington and Ralph L. Gillen, *The Business Representative in Washington* (Washington, D.C.: The Brookings Institution, 1962), p. 32.

be rewritten and resubmitted. Representatives facilitate visits from member school officials and faculty by making reservations, arranging appointments with government officials, giving them scouting reports, and providing them with a base of operations out of the Washington office. Some offices even have hotels reserve rooms on a retainer basis so that accommodations are always available, even at the height of the convention season. There is little of great political moment that takes place while the representatives tend to these duties. Invariably, they pick up scattered bits of gossip and political intelligence, but not the kind of intelligence collected or processed in a way that makes it the raw material for political action. Although all the representatives keep an eye on legislative developments, this kind of intelligence gathering is confined primarily to the major associations and the more politically assertive members of the state offices and small associations.[d]

The limitations of the small Washington outposts are not confined to the higher education community but apply as well to representatives in other interest areas. Typically these offices are staffed by one man, or a single man representing several organizations. The demands of their job make them exceptionally versatile in the range of duties they perform. They represent the group's interests before both Congress and the agencies, troubleshoot, negotiate grievances, carry out chores, and supply favors for constituents, and, in general, act as "listening posts" in Washington. Overt political action is restricted to acting as a watchdog for their members' interests. When trouble arises, they sound the alarm and then step aside and let the membership communicate directly with Congress. To reduce the burden this diversified activity places on them, they frequently collaborate with representatives of organizations that share similar concerns and problems.[6]

One newcomer to Washington represented an individual university and explained what he had to learn before he could effectively combine his commission to serve as both grantsman and political operator.

Well, I'm a newcomer to Washington, so I'm just getting oriented to the city, and trying to get acquainted with the decision-makers, people in higher education, and in the education business, as well as learning something about the legislative process, and working with our state delegation. I'm expected to do both legislative and agency work, so I'll be working with the congressional

---

[d] Seeking political intelligence is probably the most common kind of activity for Washington representatives of all kinds. Ebersole notes in his discussion of church lobbying in Washington that "if one were to judge by the unanimity with which it is acknowledged, watching legislative proceedings might be considered the most important activity of church lobbyists. They do not all watch the same legislation; they do not watch with equal efficiency; but they all 'watch' legislative proceedings." Luke Ebersole, *Church Lobbying in the Nation's Capital* (New York: Macmillan Company, 1951), p. 76.

delegation, as well as working on grant proposals. I have handled some pro-posals, although they've been pretty much limited to large proposals in specific areas exceeding a hundred thousand dollars. I've also tried to track down proposals, find out why they were rejected, as well as find out about form, content, or presentation of proposals.

Lewis Anthony Dexter argues that the main responsibility of these men is the "achievement of what are in the broad sense political purposes for his client. He knows that, to the limit of his time and skills, and ethical obligations, he should consider whatever techniques and access routes will be useful to the client; and within the limits of what is practical, he is prepared to tell his client when he lacks the most relevant kind of knowledge or the appropriate technical skills." [7] In day-to-day terms this responsibility involves many of the tasks of the education representative, as pointed out by one state system representative.

Well, I do a lot of things. I maintain contacts with agencies about their long-range planning and future programs. I disseminate the printed information poured out by the agencies, seek import clearances on special equipment, mostly for our scientists, clear up immigration problems, recruit speakers, birddog proposals, do some faculty recruiting, and do what I can for good will. I also try to sensitize our congressmen to the fact that our university does exist, and talk to them from time to time about matters in which they have expressed an interest. Communications works both ways, of course. I try to get our faculty aware of legislation, assist in the preparation of testimony, seek out prospects for various advisory and grant review panels. I watch the expiration dates, try to match up the interests with those of our faculty, and try to get them placed on these panels. That's how you get ahead in the world. We'd like to infiltrate the self-perpetuation directorate from California and the East Coast which dominates these review committees.

In view of the university administration to whom this representative was responsible, the main techniques and access routes for promoting the broad political interests of the university involved fairly routine service chores. But it also involved efforts to ascertain the long-term program plans of the major funding agencies and to infiltrate the strategic proposal review-ing panels. In addition, he was expected to cultivate the state delegation in a regular manner, not necessarily to try to influence every piece of education legislation, but to establish cordial relations—access—in the event sufficiently vital interests became involved.

Interest Group Diplomacy

The diplomatic or ambassadorial functions of the Washington representa-tives involve a strong dose of plain getting along with their colleagues.

In a more fundamental way, the representatives are responsible for keeping vigilant surveillance on developments affecting their client's interests, reporting these developments back, and where feasible and appropriate mobilizing cooperative action with other similarly interested members of the education community.[e] In a political setting that puts a high premium on hard political intelligence and where cooperative efforts are regarded as the preferred mode of political action, it is incumbent upon the representative to keep open as many channels for access and political intelligence as possible. Many of the education representatives, particularly those who have come to Washington in recent years, explained that they had been charged with serving as liaison with the Washington higher education community, the executive agencies, and their counterparts in the other associations and state offices. One director of a federal relations operation started in 1968 explained that his office was to (1) provide a mechanism for assessing the views and opinions of the membership in the field; (2) establish liaison with congressional staffs and open channels for information prior to legislative action; (3) maintain contacts with executive branches like the Office of Education, Department of Justice, and the National Institutes of Health, and keep the membership informed on developments within the various agencies; and (4) simply keep the membership informed about guidelines, administrative regulations, and deadlines.

The impressive point about the diplomatic functions of the Washington representative, both for higher education and other interest areas, is the sheer multitude of relationships the representative must establish and maintain. He is like a centrally located switching mechanism processing incoming information from colleagues, government, and his membership, analyzing and categorizing it, and sending it out again to the appropriate recipient. In addition, he is frequently called upon to assist in orienting his members to the Washington higher education and political community in much the manner of the legation's handling of a trade delegation familiarizing itself with a foreign market.

One commuter representative from a large midwestern university explained how his school had appointed a new president, a political scientist

---

[e] Cherington and Gillen, writing about the role of the business representative in Washington, suggest that "just as national interests change from time to time, company interests may, at one point in time, be primarily commercial but, at other times, involve political or legislative matters, dealings with executive agencies, or top level policy determination. The successful Washington representative must be able to handle all of these functions, as must the ambassador at the international level. Both must know public officials professionally and socially and both must know other representatives (the diplomatic community) intimately" (*The Business Representative in Washington* (Washington, D.C.: The Brookings Institute, 1962), p. 14). See also, Donald R. Hall, *Cooperative Lobbying: The Power of Pressure* (Tucson: University of Arizona Press, 1969).

with a traditional background in international relations, but who had little practical understanding of domestic politics. He admitted that it was probably a minor incident, but as preparation for assuming his new position, the representative arranged two hectic days for the new president in Washington. He set up meetings with education association officials, government and agency bureaucrats, and wound up with a combined luncheon with the state congressional delegation. "After two days of that," the representative explained, "he seemed ecstatic over having opened up contact with the Washington part of higher education and wanted me to get him active in the associations so he'd have some excuse to come to Washington. He decided he wanted to be active in the higher education establishment. I was satisfied that I had alerted him to an appreciation of the stakes involved in Washington, but I don't feel that this awareness has really penetrated down through the rest of the university administration."

While acting as tour director for visiting university presidents may not be the stuff of a representative's daily activities, this kind of intermediary or ambassadorial function does indicate the importance of this role. Diplomatic skills are particularly important in a developing interest group that is as decentralized as American higher education, as persistent in its insistence on the virtues of institutional autonomy, and is as subject to informal rather than formal norms, structures, and contacts. Until 1960 the various interests within the higher education community showed few instances of collective political efforts. Only since 1960 have these often conflicting interests acknowledged the advantages of a consensual approach to congressional and administrative policy makers. Washington representatives have played an increasingly important part in seeking out points of common interest and submerging dissensual positions that threatened to undermine efforts at policy agreements. For example, during the 1960 discussions about the continuation of the College Housing Loan Programs and other alternative measures for supporting college housing and academic construction, sharp splits among the members of the higher education community frustrated efforts to settle on common legislative priorities. It was embarrassingly clear that the Washington representatives were unable to tell sympathetic congressional leaders and administration officials where their constituents stood on the various options under consideration. Moreover, they did not feel they could presume to speak for their membership in the absence of such positions.

Under pressure from interested congressional leaders, and painfully aware that higher education was fast alienating its supporters in Congress, the executive secretaries of the major associations took the initiative and quickly forged a bill (without the usual canvass of membership opinion) that blunted the obstacles to a single, coherent higher education position.[8] Much of the credit for hammering out the consensual approach goes to the American Council, which not only managed to isolate the most divisive issues thwarting passage of proposed legislation, but by 1963 was able to speak for most of the major interests in testimony before congressional committees.[9]

These kinds of diplomatic activities take on added importance in the broader context of Washington representation. Increasingly, relations seem to be fairly long term and generally cooperative among groups sharing the same or similar interests. One empirical exploration of the nature and character of group relationships in Washington found that there was very limited movement of groups into and out of the interest group system, enduring policy preferences of groups over many years, the dominance of some policy sectors by groups of a single type, and restricted competition among groups.[10] The most recurrent theme in the analysis of these groups was "the notion of 'order' in the universe of active interest groups at the congressional level. The interview data showed there is much cooperation among group leaders, but it is carried on chiefly by informal rather than formal methods. This informal relating of group to group helps to explain the order among the hundreds of active groups." [11] In addition, respondents indicated that shared policy preferences tended to promote cooperation among groups more than any other factor.

Efforts by interest groups to maintain "order" in the political setting by minimizing conflict and emphasizing informal cooperation is fundamental to understanding the diplomatic functions performed by the Washington representatives. There are at least two distinctive levels for keeping up these exchanges, the first at the level of regular and day-to-day contacts, the second at the policy levels of the major associations. The respective levels are reflected most clearly in the semi-formal institutions of the twice-monthly meeting of the Governmental Relations Luncheon Group and the once-a-month meeting of the Higher Education Secretariat in the offices of ACE president, Logan Wilson (see page 104).

The Governmental Relations Luncheon Group originated as a small, restricted luncheon meeting during the Korean War to provide a regular means of information exchange among the members of the community. Until recently the Luncheon Group met at the Brookings Institution, but since late 1970 it has met at the fashionable La Provencal. The group has expanded in size, reflecting the same expansion in the number of higher education representatives in the city. No longer does it afford the opportunity for consideration of controversial issues or for important decision making. It is now used primarily as a regular opportunity to find out what's going on between government and higher education. In providing this opportunity, the luncheon is of particular value to those small associations and individual offices that cannot sustain the intelligence-gathering resources of the major associations. Both the diversity of membership and its size were reflected in late 1974 when there were close to 100 members listed as participants.

The fact that the group diminished in importance as a place for hammering out policy and strategy is further reflected in the fact that while executive secretaries of the major associations were listed as members, they have tended to forego these meetings with increasing regularity. In their stead, they send some lower-echelon staff member. For example, one officer of the American Council on Education noted that former Federal Relations Director Jack Morse no longer attended the meetings regularly and felt that, if only as a public relations gesture, ACE should be represented at this kind of general gathering of educational interests.

With rare exceptions, the representatives felt that the relationships within the higher education community were harmonious and almost devoid of rancor or overt personal feuds and animosities. The basis for this reaction stems largely from the kinds of relationships promoted by meetings like the Luncheon Group. Where the exchange of information is the primary concern and strategic and policy decisions are taken elsewhere for resolution, controversial issues do not drive wedges between different parts of the community. One state office association representative captured the feeling of many of her counterparts when she described the Luncheon Group as a

fine place for trading information and rumors, as well as being a sounding board for ideas and opinions. Actually, the fact of getting together for lunch was not nearly as important as making contacts with people who might be of future service or information, and who were involved in similar activities.

Another state office representative observed that she did not see "any cutthroat attitudes in the Washington higher education community. Because we all have common interests, there is a willingness to exchange information quite freely."

Yet if the representatives from the smaller associations and individual offices are the special beneficiaries of such information-exchange meetings, representatives more concerned about broader policy and strategic considerations tend to be more restive about such open forums. Several small association members complained that the Luncheon Group was no longer by invitation only, but simply a matter of paying $3.50 to reserve a seat at the restaurant. A federal relations expert from one of the major associations was even more emphatic in his skepticism about the value of such meetings.

I feel there is a definite problem of communication. I don't think that the prevailing view that the regular luncheon contact and geographical proximity at Dupont Circle, and other frequent contacts, provide the basis for general harmony among the associations. I doubt that they really work because I've seen feelings of dissatisfaction and frustration of people trying to keep on top of problems but were confused about details as well as the overall concerns of higher education. That seems to be why people come out of the meetings much more dissatisfied than they were pleased.

His reaction was distinctively in the minority, but still is understandable in terms of the differing needs of the clientele for such knowledge and information. The offices of individual schools and the small associations have neither the contacts nor the staff and expertise to compile intelligence, interpret the fine points of federal policies, or the stature to recommend courses of action. Because they are primarily geared to serving their clients in federal as opposed to legislative interest, but are simply not the raw material upon which political decisions can be reached and carried out. In contrast, such frustrations are more likely to be the lot of representatives within the major associations, and those other offices where their executive officers through preference and personality play a more active political role. While any information they pick up at such gatherings might benefit their members, it is not always as clear what it all means in policy or political terms and such open meetings are not the ideal place to thresh out such questions.

Influencing Policy

The most important function performed by the Washington representative is the effort to influence the creation, implementation, and administration of policies affecting higher education. The techniques employed by the education representatives differ little from those of their counterparts in other interest areas. They include direct participation in the drafting of legislation, personal solicitation of policy makers, indirect contacts by the membership, letter and telegram campaigns, and contacts with program administrators.

One difficulty in talking about the role of the representative in influencing policy is that influence becomes synonymous with lobbying, and lobbying immediately evokes such negative connotations and protests of innocence that both terms become impaired in their analytical utility. Attempts to exert influence over the various aspects of the policy process rest at the heart of the representative's commission to look out for the interests of his constituents and to the best of his ability provide them with the access and techniques with which to further these interests. Lobbying is simply a specific kind of effort to influence policy, and in spite of a variety of definitions, it still remains fairly limited in its scope. In its broadest use, "lobbyist" is frequently used interchangeably with the term "pressure group" to mean any organization or person that acts to influence the decisions of Congress or the administrative agencies. More narrowly, lobbyist means any person who, on behalf of some other person or group and usually for pay, attempts to influence legislation through direct contacts with legislators. Finally, the term denotes anyone who is required to register or report on his spending under the terms of the Federal Regulation of Lobbying Act of 1946.[f]

Washington representatives as a group, particularly those as fastidious as in the higher education community, are especially uneasy about being called lobbyists.[g] There are three basic reasons for higher education's sensitivity to references about their lobbying activities. First, the unfortunate connotations associated with lobbying, particularly the image of the high-geared pressure group exerting force on the hapless legislator, still persists among many educators with limited political experience. To them the pressure group evokes a very real picture of unsavory behavior directed against the public interest; and the whole purpose of higher education is seen as the antithesis of such self-serving behavior. The quick retorts and clarifications that they are not lobbyists reflect their desire for a disinterested political identity that is compatible with the purportedly disinterested pursuit of knowledge that is the basic goal of higher education.

Second, and closely related to the first point, is the fact that higher education is a fairly well isolated interest area in Washington. It has few or no visible competitors or allies outside higher education, so its contacts are largely internal. The representatives have few opportunities to compare their activities with those of their counterparts in other Washington offices. The only model that has any relevance is that of the high-pressure lobbyist. There is simply no clearly defined image of the general-purpose representative working in the interests of constituents with few or no political sanctions that might be levied on hostile decision makers. The final reason for eschewing identification as lobbyists is the desire not to run afoul of the legal provisions designed to inhibit the more blatant forms of interest group

---

[f] *Legislators and Lobbyists,* 2d ed. (Congressional Quarterly Service, May, 1968), p. 4. The law stipulates that anyone, either on his own or through any agent or employee directly or indirectly solicits, collects, or receives money or any other thing of value to be used principally to aid, or the principal purpose of which person is to aid, in the accomplishment of any of the following purposes: (a) The passage or defeat of any legislation by the Congress of the United States. (b) To influence, directly or indirectly, the passage or defeat of any legislation by the Congress of the United States. PL 79–601; Sec. 307. A 1954 Supreme Court decision further restricted the scope of the registration law by upholding its constitutionality by restricting its applicability to "direct communication with Members of Congress." *U.S.* v. *Harriss,* 347 U.S. 612 (1954).

[g] Educators are not the only ones who feel this way. For example, business representatives who took part in a roundtable discussion of Washington representation were particularly wary about being called lobbyists. They protested the connotations carried by the term and commented that their employers were reluctant to have them register as lobbyists for fear of jeopardizing the corporate image. Cherington and Gillen, *The Business Representative,* pp. 13, 46, 50.

activity. The 1946 registration law is so specific that it offers no real inhibition on the influence activities of higher education. Because it has been narrowly construed to mean direct contacts with legislators, and because relatively few higher education representatives deal directly with congressmen, only one representative felt compelled to register under the provisions of the law.

A second legal inhibition, however, has proved a much more potent restraint on the representatives. Section 501(c)3 of the Internal Revenue Code stipulates that a tax-exempt organization, including education institutions or organizations, shall lose its tax-exempt status if any "substantial part" of its activities constitutes "carrying out propaganda, or otherwise attempting, to influence legislation," or if it should "participate in, or intervene in (including the publishing or distributing of statements), any political campaign on behalf of any candidate for public office." [12] A parallel provision, Section 170(c), denies a deduction from income taxes for donors to institutions that violate these restrictions. Higher education representatives are extremely wary about the amount of time they spend in what could be considered efforts to influence legislation.[13] Even though the question of what constitutes "substantial" time in lobbying activities has not been satisfactorily determined, most education representatives (with several prominent exceptions) are very circumspect about their activities in this area because of the potentially high and intolerable costs to both their constituents and those making financial contributions to their members or association.

Interestingly, the 1946 registration act serves a rather unique function in the political world of the higher education representative, by providing him with a concrete definition of lobbying against which he can compare his own activities. When most Washington representatives, not just those from higher education, claim they are not lobbyists, what they mean is that by and large they do not directly solicit congressmen. Since they do not in fact contact congressmen with any great frequency, they are able to square their activities with the legal strictures and at the same time avoid the taint connoted by the use of lobbying to describe their activities. By these criteria, the two leading business organizations, the national Chamber of Commerce and the National Association of Manufacturers both have been extremely active in trying to influence legislation even though both groups contend that they are not lobbying organizations subject to the 1946 lobbying law.[h]

---

[h] *Legislators and Lobbyists,* p. 8. Among the sample of Washington lobbyists, many spent most of their time sending and receiving communications, most of which they did in the seclusion of their own offices; some communications were passed through personal conversations with members of Congress or other government decision makers, but these consumed little time. Entertainment was used infrequently as a mode of influence, and when contacts are needed with decision makers, lobbyists will often spend more time with the staff or legislative or administrative assistants than with the decision maker himself. Milbrath, *The Washington Lobbyists,* pp. 115–21.

This rather ingenuous and convoluted interpretation of lobbying activity, however, does not obscure the point that direct contacts with decision makers—congressmen—are not the only, or even the best, ways to represent the interests of clients in Washington. Perhaps the most direct form of policy influence by higher education representatives is direct participation in the drafting, revision, and amendment of proposed legislation. It differs from lobbying in the sense that most often such participation is at the invitation of policy makers and takes place in a cooperative rather than an adversary relationship.

For example, the former president of the Council of Graduate Schools played a prominent role in drafting the legislation that led to creation of the Foundation on the Arts and Humanities. The federal relations officer of the Association of American Colleges (AAC) was instrumental in drafting an amendment to an early version of a proposed institutional grants bill that changed the formula for the distribution of funds in a way that benefited the smaller liberal arts colleges. Jack Morse, federal relations director of the American Council on Education, has worked extensively in the preparation of higher education legislation. He has been consulted and involved in the Tax Reform Act of 1969, proposals for revision of copyright laws, questions of unemployment relating to university employees, and the 1972 education amendments.

Another aspect of direct contacts that have the effect of influencing policy involves the more restricted, less regular contacts of Washington representatives with their state delegations in Congress. These personal contacts look much more like the activities defined as lobbying than do generalized efforts to influence policy because they do in fact involve personal contacts with law makers. Representatives from the state offices and state systems have actively cultivated their state delegations. Although the total number of legislators may be small, there is at least some assurance that the representatives will have access to the members of the delegation and that some members of the group may hold strategic legislative positions.[1]

A commuter representative from one of the large midwestern universities explained that the associations did not have a single vote on Capitol Hill.

Several months ago I was having lunch with a congressman who really cared about his state university. But he was incensed at the activities going on at the other schools around the country. He candidly told me that they were intentionally out to bomb Harvard and Columbia. So, you see, if I do have any

---

[1] The state offices also have a rather unique legal status. Public colleges and universities are exempt from the federal income tax because they are appendages of the states or their instrumentalities that are exempt from tax on a constitutional basis.

influence in this respect, it's probably limited to our state delegation. But even that's far more than the associations can provide.

The commuter representative from the University of Iowa spent about 65 per cent of his working time on congressional relations. He spent the remainder doing liaison work with federal agencies and private foundations. He started work in 1969 and visited the Iowa delegation about every six weeks. These visits put him in sufficiently regular contact with the congressmen to make clear to them the impact the proposed Tax Reform Act of 1969 would have on the university, as well as to alert them to steps taken on campus to control campus unrest, and to stress the significance for the university of the proposed Department of Health, Education, and Welfare budget.[14]

Princeton University's representative, also a commuter since the summer of 1970, indicated openly that the Congress was not the sole or necessarily the most critical point for trying to influence policy. He explained that "we feel there's been a change in the federal power structure. It's clear that many decisions are being made in the Executive Office Building —more than were made five or ten years ago. We want to recognize that." [15] One instance of action taken on this assumption was arrangement of a luncheon for William G. Bowen, provost of Princeton and a specialist in education economics, with the chief of the human resources programs division of the Office of Management and Budget. Efforts to communicate with and influence the thinking of men in the executive branch, most importantly in the offices where budgets are hammered out, are at least as significant a political activity as letter campaigns enlisting the support or opposition of lawmakers on legislative proposals. It is not considered lobbying, however, because it does not involve direct contacts with lawmakers, is a low-visibility activity, and tests of effectiveness are far more subtle and long term than straightforward acceptance or rejection of legislation.

Far and away the most recurrent kinds of efforts to influence policy are by the members and constituents of the representatives themselves. The representative alerts and frequently mobilizes his people, but the actual communications and contacts ultimately come from the field. Milbrath found that the Washington lobbyists in his sample acted as advocates of a particular position by arranging to have messages come from those to whom decision makers were likely to be receptive. They also wrote and arranged for presentation of testimony by their clients before congressional committees. Such efforts at indirect influence as testimony by prominent individuals and letter and telegram campaigns from the membership are the favored devices of the Washington higher education community. There is a general feeling that policy preferences are best expressed by those affected by the policy, and a more specific feeling that efforts to influence policy in this manner get around injunctions against lobbying. One officer of a major association explained:

Neither Jack nor I see ourselves as lobbyists. Oh, we talk to congressmen like Daddario and Mosher on specific matters like the Miller bill, but we prefer to use our college presidents. For example, I will send out telegrams to our state directors to get their own president's veto of the education appropriations bill. We have taken part in such minor kinds of legislation as social security benefits for ordained ministers, something which is really confined to our category of schools . . . Certainly nothing major.

He did not feel that their tax-exempt status had inhibited their activity, but did admit they kept a pretty close watch on the amount of time they spent on political activities.

The representative's most recurring political role is to facilitate or expedite efforts by his constituents to influence policy. He learns when hearings are planned on legislation of interest to his clients, tries to get a slot at the hearings, helps research and draft testimony, and enlists impressive spokesmen to present the membership's case. Most representatives prefer that contacts with decision-makers are made by their members, except when it is necessary to respond to a specific situation in which it is inconvenient or impossible for this to be done by someone not on the paid staff of the association. Quite often members of Congress, usually through their staffs, initiate requests for information, comments, suggestions, but this grows up through personal acquaintance at hearings and other less formal contacts.

In short, reaching a point where it is possible to exert influence on behalf of a constituency depends on patience, availability to decision makers when called upon, and the careful cultivation of acquaintances and contacts so that when policy questions do come up, the representative is called upon to at least express an opinion. These patterns of access and personal influence look very little like the stereotype of lobbying, for they are virtually devoid of the kinds of threats and sanctions that are implicit in the common image of the legislator-lobbyist relationship. But in the broadest political sense these patterns are still means of influencing policy by the Washington representative (and his constituents) on behalf of those whose interests he is responsible for protecting and promoting.

The final point in this description of what the Washington representatives do is to point out that the bulk of political activity is carried out by the major associations, with the small associations and state office representatives playing a more sporadic role limited primarily to their own state delegations. Even amidst this division of political labor, the striking point is that nearly all the representatives had so many demands on their time and resources that it was very hard for them to devote a great deal of time

to cultivating the Congress or key agencies. If there is any one characteristic of association life that inhibits the representative from legislative
activity, it is the plethora of services demanded by clients. Only the American Council and the junior colleges have the resources to support a separate staff devoted wholly to political work—and even these staffs are
hard pressed to do all they feel needs to be done. In another respect, however, it is hardly surprising that the associations are the locus of most of
the direct and indirect efforts to influence policy for there are more of them,
they can sustain at least minimal division of labor within the organization,
and through their relatively long tenure in Washington they have attained
some degree of recognition and legitimacy from policy makers.

The persistent view of the lobbyist as the vanguard of the powerful
pressure group has stultified understanding of the interest group process by
focusing too narrowly on one particular kind of activity at the expense of
a host of other activities. Hard lobbying, the constant solicitation of congressmen, the letter campaigns, campaign support, and the unspoken
threat of defeat at the polls, is the activity that keeps alive the stereotyped
lobbyist. But this intensive activity is really the most visible peak of actions
and relationships that have taken place in far less dramatic circumstances.
Peak activity occurs at the critical points in the legislative process, and it is
here that the lobby professional takes over tactical decisions and vote-
counting. However, these professionals make up only a small part of the
interest group representatives in Washington. It is the representatives who
do much of the routine communication and mobilization that give continuity from one peak effort to the next. Where lobbying in the sense of intense
efforts to influence legislation at strategic junctures in the policy process is
meant to advance new measures and protect old privileges, much of the
representatives' work is aimed at supplementing these efforts and, in addition, exploiting advantages that already exist.

Viewed in this perspective, it is possible to modify the mechanical
image of the relentless pressure group led by powerful lobbyists putting the
squeeze on the hapless legislator. The picture that emerges instead is that
of a group of men and a few women looking a great deal like their fellow
representatives in business, labor, farm, and service associations maintaining offices in Washington. They are limited in money, time, and resources,
and are occasionally ill-understood by the very people they represent. Much
of their time is spent in routine communications and other administrative
chores; most have few contacts with members of Congress. Their basic
responsibility is to alert a sometimes heedless membership to its interests,
or apparent interests, in pending or existing legislation and try to get it to
act on these interests by making direct contact with policy makers. There
is a powerful consensus among Washington representatives that they make
a far less impressive case on a particular issue than do those in the or-

ganization directly affected by it. To adopt a restrictive understanding of lobbying is really to miss the richness of the ways in which Washington representatives work directly and indirectly to influence policy. There is no question that the higher education representatives in looking out for the interests of their clients are trying to influence policy in a variety of ways. If they were not, they would be remiss in their responsibilities as representatives.

Notes

1. Lester W. Milbrath, *The Washington Lobbyists* (Chicago: Rand McNally & Company, 1936), p. 97.

2. *Digest of Educational Statistics, 1971 Edition,* table 11, p. 9.

3. Milbrath, *The Washington Lobbyists,* p. 69.

4. Lewis Anthony Dexter, *How Organizations are Represented in Washington* (Indianapolis: Bobbs-Merrill Company, 1969), p. 113.

5. Ibid., p. 130; italics in the original.

6. Milbrath, *The Washington Lobbyists,* p. 155.

7. Dexter, *How Organizations Are Represented,* p. 44; emphasis in original omitted.

8. Homer D. Babbidge and Robert M. Rosenzweig, *The Federal Interest in Higher Education* (New York: McGraw-Hill Book Company, Inc., 1962), pp. 102–113.

9. Lawrence K. Pettit, *The Politics of Federal Policymaking for Higher Education,* manuscript, chap. II, pp. 46–52.

10. Robert L. Ross, "Dimensions and Patterns of Relations among Interest Groups at the Congressional Level of Government," unpublished Ph.D. dissertation, Michigan State University, 1967.

11. Ibid., pp. 403–404.

12. 26 U.S.C. 501(c) (3).

13. 26 U.S.C. 170(c).

14. Ed Willingham, "Washington Pressures/Nation's Colleges, Universities Set Up Office to Deal with Government," *National Journal,* April 14, 1971, p. 851.

15. Quoted ibid., p. 848.

4

The Changing Political Perspectives of the Washington Representatives

Although the higher education representatives share certain characteristics and activities with Washington representatives from other interest areas, they have their own distinctive pattern of assumptions, preferences, and attitudes toward political action. Changes in the basic assumptions concerning political activity provide important signs about the transformation of the Washington higher education community from a passive to a more assertive political role. This transition has occurred with an understandable amount of soul-searching, a reluctance to acknowledge the changes in an earlier, less turbulent status quo, and the more generalized frustrations and discomforts rooted in the unsettling conditions of change. This chapter will describe the basic political perspectives of the representatives, their antecedents in political experience, and some of the important political consequences of these beliefs and assumptions.

Two events in the recent political experience of higher education provide concrete illustrations of the different aspects of style and sentiment in the Washington higher education community during the late 1960s and early 1970s. The first is the response of the representatives to efforts aimed at achieving full funding of existing education programs, and the second a proposal for the creation of separate lobbying and information organizations independent of the existing Washington establishment.

The Sullivan Proposal for a Permanent Lobbying Organization

In his report to the 1969 annual meeting of the Association of American Colleges, President Richard H. Sullivan suggested the possibility of creating two new organizations for higher education, one devoted explicitly to lobbying, the other to generating information designed to explain and clarify American higher education to the public.[1] His basic premise was that the bewildering diversity of American higher education promoted a situation where higher education was not effectively organized to achieve the broad goals that it had set for itself, nor was it sympathetically understood by the people it served.

He argued that the existing organizations had advanced the interests

61

of colleges and universities and had promoted the cause of higher education but that legal and psychological inhibitions and forces of habit and custom had limited higher education's capacity to actually "get the votes." He conceded that "on the whole, educators, by temperament and for other reasons, don't make the best lobbyists. . . . The limitations on lobbying by our present organizations, among other reasons because they are tax exempt, are reasonable." Sullivan concluded that higher education might well need a new organization, one he tentatively called "Higher Education, Inc."

It should be well staffed with effective people who take pride in getting results. Properly, it should not claim tax exemption, yet it should be well financed. This means it would have to be supported by personal, not institutional contributions. You and I and other individuals on and off campuses who believe that higher education needs more votes in Congress would, presumably, have to foot the bill for the work to get those votes. The staff of the new organization . . . should operate with the highest ethical standards, and I find no conflict between that code and expectation, on the one hand, and on the other, the activity of presenting to members of Congress, vigorously and persuasively, the case for desired legislation for the improvement of higher education.[2]

He saw the new organization as having specific value in the actual mechanics of mobilizing legislative support.

Our present structures and people in Washington do a good job in proposing language, but not as well as might be done when Congressmen or Senators start re-writing bills. We can usually get a bill introduced, but not always by just the right man. We know a lot about the committees handling legislation on higher education, but many votes in committee have gone against us. And we are not staffed for, nor are we expert in, getting the votes on the floor, or in getting the friendly Congressmen to the floor to vote. "Higher Education, Inc." could help at all those stages, and I think there may be . . . a reasonable conclusion that we need it.[3]

In addition, the new organization would work to mobilize the grassroots sentiments of those both inside and outside higher education. This mobilization and proselytization would be supplemented by a second organization, this one tax exempt, "engaged in [the] true education work [of] getting the American people to understand with more sophistication and realism the processes and institutions of higher education [as] an educational enterprise of the first magnitude." [4]

The Sullivan proposal was important for two reasons. First, it marked an unusual departure for association executives in that the president of a major association set out to analyze the political deficiencies of higher education and to offer explicit remedial measures in the form of new organizational arrangements. Second, the proposal was directed at the rank-

and-file members of the AAC, and not confined to quiet circulation in the inner confines of the Washington higher education establishment. Sullivan brought into the open some important themes in the thinking of part of the higher education community, themes that reflected a growing concern for the realities of political life and the impact of national policy on higher education. The reactions of various representatives to the proposals offer one indication of these themes in the political attitudes of the representatives.

The Emergency Committee for Full-Funding of Education Programs

The Emergency Committee for Full-Funding of Education Programs originated in the spring of 1969 when members of several education interests recognized the dire effects of budget cutbacks for all aspects of education during the last years of the Johnson administration and in the first budget of the new Nixon administration. The common sentiment was that a unified effort by education offered the only hope of restoring funds, and, in a broader sense, of dramatizing the issue of national spending priorities.

The budget requested by the Full-Funding Committee was a design of compelling imagination that meshed the different parts of the proposed spending package with little dispute. The key to the entire package was a request for a $398 million increase over the Nixon allotment for aid to school districts "impacted" by high concentrations of federal employees. Both Republican and Democratic administrations had attacked the impact aid program as a boondoggle; yet it had the irresistible appeal of funneling federal dollars into at least 385 congressional districts.[a]

In July the coalition, comprising nearly 80 education groups, persuaded the House to add $1 billion to the Office of Education appropriation for the current fiscal year. When the Senate stalled in acting on the House bill, the coalition executed a rare legislative maneuver in the House that resulted in the billion-dollar increase. In a fairly routine measure the House leadership introduced a resolution to provide stopgap spending authority for the rest of the year to agencies whose appropriations bills had not been enacted. Such resolutions ordinarily continue spending at past

---

[a] In addition, vocational education, a favorite of Republican congressmen, received a $131.5 million increase, and the various library and equipment programs an additional $110.4 million. Higher education got $73.8 million for construction and student loans. *Wall Street Journal*, January 20, 1970. Altogether the coalition requested $4.6 billion more than the administration had proposed. Unofficially, the coalition lobbyists were willing to settle for a great deal less. There was a feeling that when demands exceeded $1 billion at a single stroke, they offered a dangerous provocation to the congressional appropriations process.

levels, and it is unusual to include an increase for a specific agency. The House overrode the desires of its own powerful appropriations committee and supported the additional funds. The Senate quickly passed an identical resolution.

The appropriations battle came to a head late in January 1970, when President Nixon signed a televised veto of the $19.7 billion appropriations bill for the Departments of Labor and of Health, Education, and Welfare on the grounds that it was inflationary. The Full-Funding Committee mobilized the most intensive effort of its existence to persuade the House to override the president's veto. Professional lobbyists from the National Education Association and the AFL-CIO quarterbacked the activities of the amateur education lobbyists who flew in from all over the country. At the height of the battle there were nearly 900 educators meeting with their representatives, while others manned an elaborate whip system on the Hill and in all three House office buildings. In spite of the mobilization of grass-roots support and a disciplined, well-organized campaign, the coalition was defeated when the House failed by 52 votes to override the veto. The critical factor in the vote was Republican support, which was severely inhibited by intense White House pressure for party loyalty.[b]

Although higher education's dollar stakes in the coalition were probably smaller than any of the other major education interests, the leadership of the major associations consented to participate in the effort. The American Council circulated a letter signed by the executives of six other associations to some 450 colleges soliciting financial support for the committee.[c] One reason higher education took the unusual step of soliciting funds was the feeling of the representatives, especially those from the ACE and the Association of American Law Schools, that the committee should not accept the offer of the hardware, audio-visual, or book-publishing people to finance the operation.[d] Actual participation in the decision-making activities

---

[b] One of the professional labor lobbyists active in organizing the Full-Funding Committee's effort recalled that in frequenting the halls of Congress he had talked to some of the lobbyists from the forest products interests. When he asked how they happened to be in on the appropriations fight, they told him they had been called by the White House and reminded that they had a timber bill in the hoppers; since the White House needed the appropriations bill, the timber people had better get over to the Hill and start lobbying for it.

[c] The other associations were the Council of Protestant Colleges and Universities, the National Catholic Education Association, the NASULGC, the AASCU, the AAC, and the American Association of Colleges for Teacher Education.

[d] The Urban Coalition Action Council, a national group trying to rehabilitate the cities, and the AFL-CIO both claimed they would not participate in the lobby if it were financed by the commercial interests. None of the major parties to the coalition wanted to be linked with profit-making enterprises in which their own efforts looked like an unholy alliance with the business interests, and as such, reduced the stature and prestige of education to the level of most profit-making enterprises.

of the Full-Funding Committee was limited to a small number of men from the associations and state offices who attended the breakfast meetings of the committee's steering committee. Jack Talmadge, federal relations officer for the AAC, Frank Mensel, the federal relations man from the junior colleges, Robert Carmody from the California State Office, and Rowan Wakefield from the State University of New York Office were among the most active members from the higher education community. The ACE's Jack Morse was particularly active during the formative stages of the coalition effort and helped recruit Arthur Flemming, former HEW head in the Eisenhower administration, as committee chairman, thus giving the committee a solid bipartisan tone. The reactions of representatives to participation in the Full-Funding Committee, like their reactions to the Sullivan proposal, suggest a range and diversity of attitudes toward higher education's political role that sorts into three basic themes: traditional, pragmatic, and activist.

The Traditional Perspective: The Unique Character of Higher Learning and the Sublimation of Political Self-Interest

It is hardly surprising that the political perspectives of the Washington representatives during a decade in which the relationship between the federal government and higher education has altered profoundly should be frequently contradictory, diverse, and ambivalent. There are, however, three discernible themes that recur in conversations with the representatives: one that minimizes the role of higher education in politics; a second that admits to such a role on a pragmatic basis; and a third that urges higher education to play a more assertive role in national politics. Rarely are these themes sharply distinguished from one another; frequently elements from each contribute to the cognitive fabric of the individual representatives. In any case, these perceptions are significant because they exert a powerful influence on the actual behavior of the representatives and on their judgments of what other strategic elites outside higher education feel constitutes legitimate and appropriate political activity for higher education.

The traditional perspective is one that is fundamental to nearly everyone involved with higher education, both within the Washington community and within the colleges and universities themselves. In essence, it holds that advanced learning has an intrinsic value for the cultural and intellectual life of society, and as such should compel the support of the major institutions, including government, of the society in which advanced education takes place. The university, as the embodiment of the higher learning, can only sustain its integrity by guarantees of academic freedom, the freedom to teach and to learn, that insulate it from external stricture and controls that would cripple its mission in the pursuit of truth.

One of the basic corollaries of this perspective is that because of its unique character, higher education does not rank on a plane with other social or political interests or institutions. The manifestation of this assumption has been the pattern of snobbish elitism that traditionally has marked some of the most prominent national universities. The impression given by these institutions was that not only did they hold a special place in the intellectual life of the nation, but their positions were so firmly assured that there were no serious questions about their basic operating premises. The student discontent of the mid- and late 1960s went a long way toward dislocating the equanimity afforded by these assumptions. At the level of national politics the best evidence of the erosion of these premises has been the belated entry of the Association of American Universities (AAU) into an active federal relations role. Prior to the 1964 Berkeley upheaval and, more painfully, the turmoil that wracked Columbia University in 1968, many of the AAU member universities were complacent in their assumption that their reputations for academic excellence and integrity were sufficient to guarantee them continued national recognition and protection from external sources of instability.

The most important political consequence of the traditional view is the assumption that when education does become involved in national politics, it must do so in a way that transcends narrow concerns of self-interest and incorporates the widest possible consideration for the national interest. In addition to this sense of patrician obligation comes a disdain for the mechanics of adversary politics, a feeling that the tedious work of engineering compromises, and that mobilizing support exists at the margins of professional dignity and propriety. The recurrent assumption has been that the resolution of political conflict and the creation of public policy is based on rational discourse and the disinterested consideration of the national interest, not from the accommodation reached amidst the rough-and-tumble of politics.

One illustration from the early 1960s of this desire to explore in public the delicate policy proposals, even to one's own potential detriment, was higher education's handling of the church-state issue during discussions of federal aid to education. The question of federal aid to church-related colleges had never been the sensitive issue in higher education that it had been at the primary and secondary levels, but spokesmen for higher education felt compelled to stake out a policy position where there was no pressure to do so. The result was that a tactically extraneous issue became an important issue for deliberation. A former member of the Office of Education concluded that this inappropriate raising of issues stemmed from the educators' "incurable urge to act as statesmen." He went on to observe that "until very recently higher education's administrators have seemed unable or unwilling to distinguish and make a rational separation between their role as educational statesmen and their role as political operators lobbying on behalf of their institutions' interests." [5]

Two veterans of higher education politics concurred on the political consequences of this style. They observed that when these spokesmen debated the possibility of aid to higher education, "they were not content to describe their needs and the most effective manner of meeting them; instead, they took on the larger issue, whether it would constitute sound public policy to meet these needs. They did not argue over their needs and interests; they argued over a broad question of public policy, in this instance, the so-called church-state issue." [e] They are careful to point out that this compulsion to take policy stands is characteristic of college administrators, rarely of the Washington representatives. The dilemma for the representative is how best to reconcile the positions of those he represents with the exigencies of Washington policy making.

The premise that policy questions merited rational, public consideration, and the decentralized character of the higher education community, created a situation where minority spokesmen were accorded an excessive amount of deference and indulgence by the community. Not surprisingly, this indulgence encumbered rather than smoothed the way for achievement of top legislative goals. Until as late as 1963, the Association of American Colleges (AAC), traditionally the most conservative of the major associations, was opposed to any kind of federal assistance. The AAC was one of the last groups to concede the desirability of federal grants for the construction of academic facilities. Its membership's traditional misgivings about governmental interference and its serious reservations about the church-state issue constrained many AAC members from endorsing a grant program. At the 1960 meeting, members expressed intense opposition to any type of federal grants. Although the AAC issued a policy statement in favor of federal aid for academic facilities, it forbade the legislative commission from committing the organization to any proposal involving grants without further reference to the entire membership.

The AAC membership had also been the locus of intense concern about the church-state issue. The small Protestant colleges, many of which

---

[e] Homer D. Babbidge and Robert M. Rosenzweig, *The Federal Interest in Higher Education* (New York: McGraw-Hill Book Company, 1962) p. 111. They add a bit caustically that "it is a little presumptuous for a group of educators to attempt—as a group—to resolve an issue such as that of Church and State *before* it comes to Congress. . . . At any rate, this self-imposed sense of corporate responsibility for having and expressing views on issues of public policy has gotten in the way of effective expression of higher-educational needs."

opposed any type of federal aid to higher education, were especially stubborn in their opposition to the allocation of tax dollars to church-related institutions. The disruptive and counterproductive nature of this kind of opposition, even when confined to a small minority within an association, surfaced in 1962 during the height of the legislative maneuvering to get a higher education facilities act out of the House Rules Committee. A group of 29 college presidents, almost all of them from small Protestant colleges, sent telegrams to the committee in opposition to a bill that provided construction grants and federal scholarships for private as well as public institutions. These schools formed the core of a dissident, conservative group within the AAC, many of whose administrators maintained rapport with conservative political groups. During hearings before the Senate Subcommittee on Education, a panel representing many of the colleges in this group testified against the higher education bill, against federal aid in principle, and in favor of tax credits.[6]

The third political consequence of the traditional perspective on politics was the failure to promote and cultivate political coalitions that embraced interests outside the immediate higher education community. The value attached to the purpose and intrinsic merit of higher education, its self-perception as acting in the broadest public interest, and the recurrent streak of independence based on the desire to perpetuate the autonomy of the higher learning have combined to create a wary, uncomfortable attitude toward political alliances with those interests whose values do not mesh with those of higher education. This inherent suspicion, bred from the attitude that self-interested, adversary politics were at best unsavory, has been reinforced by the isolation of the higher education community from other ostensibly compatible interests. For example, until the efforts of the Full-Funding Committee, educational interests had divided rather sharply along elementary-secondary and higher education lines. Few contacts existed between the two components of America's educational system. There has been no pattern of cooperation or consultation with the more liberal labor organizations on issues of common interest. And, as pointed out in the preceding chapter, the higher education representatives themselves have been isolated from their counterparts in other interest areas to the point where they rarely identify their own activities with those of a broader group of political specialists.

Several aspects of the traditional perspective still find their way into the attitudes of a minority of Washington representatives, for the most part men who are not in direct day-to-day contact with federal relations. The feeling that higher education had a responsibility to the broader aspects of public policy, plus the suspicion of coalition politics, were reflected in the reaction of a representative to the Full-Funding Committee. "I, myself," she said, "do not like the idea that higher education has linked itself with the pork barrel of impact aid. I just don't like the use of this method to pass legislation. There's always the danger of feedback or backlash on the part of Congress stemming from resentment of the intensive pressures under which they've been placed during the past several months to grant full funding of higher education programs."

Another comment by a young relations officer from a major association captures the essence of the traditional perspective: the compatibility of higher education's policy goals with the national interest; the fear of long-term losses stemming from an association with abrasive lobbying efforts; and a preference for a political style that stressed low visibility and the muting or strident policy demands. He responded to the Sullivan proposal by explaining:

I'm not really enthusiastic about education's having an independent lobbying arm. Perhaps there's a short-term advantage, but I suspect that there would be long-term losses. *It may seem old-fashioned, but I still believe that education can and should present their appeals in terms of the national interest, in terms of the benefits to young people.* Furthermore, we can't really evaluate just how effective such an organization might be. They would continually have to justify their existence. It would certainly transcend the immediate legislation at hand, and would result in excessive claims, chest-thumping, and other activities that would be designed to keep them in the public eye. I feel that this would be bad for education. There seems to be an increasing decline in sensitivity to this point; for example, ———— prefers a more active and personal style and tactics in federal relations. My own preference is for a low-key operation as long as this kind of operation can be sustained successfully. [Emphasis added.]

These same themes were reiterated by an ACE official who expressed his personal misgivings about the Full-Funding Committee.

I was skeptical of the Full-Funding Committee initially. It was nothing in particular, just that no one had done anything like it before. The committee seems to have been successful beyond most people's most optimistic hopes, but the question remains about how long they can keep it up. Furthermore, how long will Congress indulge these kinds of pressure tactics that have gone on all week? The basic question in my mind is whether you can lobby for higher education the same way you can lobby for Lockheed. You know, all the entertainments, special pleasures, and special considerations that are entailed. I'm not sure, but a growing number of associations have added federal relations offices and devoted increasing shares of their budget for this purpose. Higher education is becoming more dependent on federal money, to be sure. And like most things that you come to learn to live with, your sensitivities become dulled, almost inevitably. I regret it myself.

Another high ACE official captured the traditional perspective's assessment of coalition politics when explaining his mixed feelings about the Full-Funding Committee. He had endorsed the fund-raising letter that had circulated among the colleges and universities but was not wholly convinced about the value of higher education's participation in the coalition.

I did have misgivings about crawling into bed with so many other interests like the labor unions and the impact aid people. Now I have nothing against labor unions, but I'm just not sure about getting involved too deeply with that kind of coalition. . . . The thing that disturbs me is that the administration always seems willing to call in George Meany and the labor unions when they're discussing legislation, but not higher education. It's becoming increasingly difficult these days to convince Congress about the value of higher education to the nation and society through logical discussion.

The evolution of the higher education coalition between 1960 and 1963 with the passage of the Higher Education Facilities Act anticipated the transformation of the traditional perspectives to assumptions based far more on pragmatic than traditional ideological concerns. Accompanying these shifts in perceptions was a shift in the locus of political activity from the presidents and college administrators to the more politically attuned Washington representatives. The transition was not always an easy one or one accepted enthusiastically, as indicated by a 1962 statement by ACE president Logan Wilson.

Although I agree with our Executive Committee that it would be a mistake for us to become an action or lobbying organization as distinguished from one engaged in broader pursuits, I am of the opinion that we have an obligation to influence educational developments in the right direction. Whether we like it or not, this involves a closer and more effective liaison between educational leaders and key figures in the legislative and executive branches of government. *Neither higher education nor the government is well served when the representations being made come mainly from special interest groups which often are either ignorant of or indifferent to total needs and the priorities implicit in them.*[7]

Pragmatic Realism: Higher Education's Adaptation to New Political Relationships

Wilson's efforts to reconcile the traditional perspectives about higher education's political role with the changed political setting lies at the basis of the shift in attitude toward a more prudent and pragmatic assessment of political activity by higher education. The pragmatic realists—most of the representatives are best described this way—try to retain the assumptions about the unique character of higher education and the need to make policy through rational discourse. At the same time they strive to judge the strategic and tactical considerations of their constituents in terms of their political strengths and liabilities. The political consequences of this effort to merge new political realities with more fundamental assumptions has resulted in a characteristic diffidence and reserve about more aggressive forms of political activity, plus a recurrent emphasis on the tactical needs for coalitions in order to speak to policy makers with a united front.

This reserved approach to political action is based largely on the assumptions of the traditional perspective. These assumptions are that higher education has an integrity of its own that is jeopardized by political action, and that when higher education does become politically involved, it should do so in a rational rather than an adversary manner. One federal relations officer captured this sentiment when commenting on the Sullivan proposal. He admitted that he had no really clear feelings, but in considering the experience of the Full-Funding Committee, believed that a rational case could be made through reasoned discussion and the presentation of facts. "At least that was the atmosphere we lived in until 1969. The question is whether education's case is so weak that if we are able to survive, we must change our tactics and move into some form of permanent lobbying."

An observer outside the immediate higher education community commented on the diffidence higher education had shown in the full-funding operation. "As far as I can see," he remarked, "all it did was show how little influence higher education really had, both in the amount of money involved and their overall role in the committee. They did not press for more money, but sat back, grateful for the litte bit they were getting. That's what I mean by lacking energy or political commitment to improve their relative position."

The American Council's federal relations director, Jack Morse, responded to the intensified effort of the Full-Funding Committee by giving serious consideration to withdrawing from the coalition in the wake of the override battle. He initially supported the joint venture because he viewed American education as a total system and philosophically believed that education, as a totality, was not one in which one part should compete with another, as had been the typical case in appropriations fights. He was not, however, pleased with the more strident efforts of the Full-Funding Committee and threatened the coalition leadership that he would pull the ACE out if they did not stop using "strong arm tactics." Although he maintained his belief in the concept of a unified appropriations process, he was fearful of a congressional backlash, particularly since the coalition was a strange one and involved the impact aid people.ᶠ He was caught in the

---

ᶠ The fear of antagonizing congressmen through the tactics of the committee was not fanciful. Ohio Republican William H. Ayres called the lobbying effort "a disgrace to the good name of education." *Washington Post,* January 29, 1970. The actions of the committee also had the effect of incurring the wrath of Edith Green, the one legislator higher education could ill afford to alienate since her subcommittee handled most higher education legislation. In a statement on the House floor she expressed

position of having to defend participation to the ACE Board, which demanded a more philosophical explanation of the nature of the alliance, and not the pragmatic political explanation of it. Thus, in spite of the efforts of the Washington representatives to inject a measure of pragmatism into their activities, they are still constrained in how far they can go by their governing boards and their constituents. And these are the individuals most likely to stick to the more traditional assumptions about higher education's place in politics.

The reaction of the Full-Funding Committee's professional lobbyists to higher education's role illuminates the nature of the political transformation experienced by it. One of the coalition's organizers remarked that the American Council's involvement at the forefront of the initial proposal for higher education's involvement would not have happened several years before. "They seemed a lot less squeamish about it," he remarked, "but they still have a long way to go." Several organizers concurred in observing that higher education's participation in full-tilt politics was probably an unsettling one, but credited it with extensive cooperation and assistance. "I give higher education credit," said one organizer, "for submerging their interests to the broader goals of the coalition. They never budged, never moved an inch, and all the time seemed to feel it was worthwhile." One labor lobbyist observed:

When higher education agreed to incorporate themselves into the committee, they had to make the hard political decision that once they were in, they had to stay in. I don't think they were used to this pure political style. It involved rough and tumble politics, hard-nosed tough lobbying, and I don't think higher education over operated like that. The fight over the veto was not really planned as a giant television spectacular; the initial response was to make the appropriations process more responsive to the needs of education. We had no intention of knocking over the Appropriations Committee, but from a small operation, we suddenly found ourselves in the major leagues. We were used to it, but higher education wasn't. Coalitions for us are nothing new because we've been strong proponents of coalition efforts. I had the impression that the higher education guys were uncomfortable. They play a different ballgame than we do, mostly in the states with the governors.

---

her concern about the "educational-industrial complex in the United States that is increasing in size and strength. The military budget has $80 billion in it. In the United States today at the Federal and state and local levels we are spending about $60 billion on education." *New York Times*, November 3, 1969. She charged that corporations and consulting groups with a stake in the school market were the real powers behind the education lobby and argued that "there is an inherent danger if we allow decisions to be made on the educational priorities of this country by the pressures of lobby groups that have a personal and financial stake in the outcome." *Wall Street Journal*, January 20, 1970. Jack Morse was in a particularly delicate position because he gained his initial political experience as a staff member on Mrs. Green's subcommittee.

Another representative captured the flavor of the pragmatic perspective when he conceded that there was probably a need for some kind of permanent lobbying organization, but that it would entail political costs.

First of all, it would destroy the aura of disinterest and detachment which has been one of higher education's most respected points. Second of all, it would become identified as a lobby group, which in itself would be undesirable, and which would require a public relations operation managed with great care. Furthermore, the very complexity of federal relations and the variety of higher education associations make it difficult to define what such an organization could and should do. Basically, of course, the job would be to get results in terms of legislation, but I'm still wary and cautious about the kinds of involvement that involve pressuring Congress.

The pragmatic realists, while they share much with their more prudent counterparts, still take a much less philosophical view of political involvement, and a much more analytical one that weighs the strengths and weaknesses of higher education's political position against anticipated gains and losses. The long experience of the National Association of State Universities and Land-Grant Colleges in state and national politics has made this association's representatives some of the most astute realists in the Washington community. One representative claimed he was skeptical of the Full-Funding Committee from the beginning and questioned the wisdom of sending droves of college presidents to the Hill.

The result is bound to be a backlash of ill-will which is simply not the way to get legislation passed . . . We just didn't care for the tactics, particularly linking aid to higher education to impact aid. We saw little that the Full-Funding Committee could do that the association couldn't do itself. *Besides they picked poor points to generate tests of strength with the administration; those kinds of power plays that should have been used as last resorts were instead used as part of the overall strategy involved in trying to get full-funding. I suspect that the long-term losses will probably offset any short-range gains they might make.* [Emphasis added.]

The same representative gave a predictable response to the Sullivan proposal.

No, thanks. We don't lobby. We don't feel that education should have to use that method. Consequently, we don't feel it's necessary to lobby like the Full-Funding Committee. Congress is not made up of a bunch of morons, although it may have been in the past. Most of them are fairly intelligent and are willing to listen to good ideas. We find it much more effective to approach problems in a low-key manner that does not offend the taste and judgment of the individual congressman.

Another representative from a major association was especially vehement in his distaste for the efforts of the Full-Funding Committee, again in terms of some pragmatic assessment of the uses and abuses of existing political resources. He first raised the question of how long the "emergency" was going to last, and pointed out that an accommodation would have to be reached at some point. Whether that point would come along the line of impact aid or whether it was really beneficial to use that as the key-stone of the coalition remained to be seen. "Furthermore," he went on,

> the style used by the committee was primitive at best, and probably self-defeating—somewhere along the line of the public highway contractors. It was totally unsophisticated and very costly in terms of good will lost as well as respect and prestige subverted by some rather crass lobbying techniques. . . . Higher education just cannot lobby like the unions or big business. In Congress there is often a self-selection process at work where the people who end up on the education committees with which education has the most contact are people who are aware and conscious of higher education's role in the country. It would be both demeaning to higher education, and to the congressmen them-selves to embark on this rather crude kind of lobbying. It's necessary to main-tain an appropriate style in presentations for higher education to Congress. . . . Ultimately, education has the right to depend upon the sympathies of Congress. In terms of assets, higher education has had a history of knowledge, credibility, and honesty in the presentation of its case. . . . This kind of ap-proach makes it possible for a Congressman to enhance his own reputation through identification with a popular cause—or what used to be a popular cause—that would pay dividends in terms of his own prestige and good will. Full-funding, on the other hand, tends to compromise the image, thus jeop-ardizing these critical but intangible resources.

The shift in the responsibility for the articulation of higher education's political demands from the administrators to the Washington representa-tives, and the concurrent shift from a traditional to a pragmatic orientation, have fostered the second political consequence, an emphasis on coalition efforts in presenting policy arguments to decision makers. The insistence of top association officials on the need for a unified higher education com-munity has clear roots in the bumbling approach to federal aid in the early 1960s. Because the political signals were still called mainly by the college presidents, the Washington representatives were severely handicapped in taking any independent action without seeking the collective judgments of their constituents. Consequently, they were unable to tell interested con-gressional leaders and administrative officials where their memberships stood on the various alternatives and did not feel that they were authorized to negotiate in the absence of such positions.[8] This indecisiveness prompted one of higher education's proponents, Senator Joseph S. Clark, to chide the educators for their paralysis. He conceded that the higher education community was made up of a heterogeneous cluster of interests that made it difficult to unite on a legislative program, but raised the question of whether the existing organizations were set up to do the necessary job of working out a proper plan for federal aid and then lobbying vigorously for it. He went on to ask:

Would it not be desirable to organize an *ad hoc* committee of leading educators and other citizens who are convinced of the need for federal aid so that, when they meet, they need not argue whether, but only how? Let us remember that educators are not monks who a take a vow of poverty, both for themselves and for the institutions they serve. They, too, are American citizens with the right, indeed the duty, to petition for redress of grievances and to indicate to their elected representatives how they would like those grievances redressed.[9]

The representatives realized that they were witnesses to the erosion of support by influential political leaders in the administration and Congress through their persistent refusal to commit themselves to policy positions in the absence of approved positions formally adopted by their entire memberships. Subsequently, several key association executive secretaries met with Senator Clark, made it clear that they were not speaking with the sanction of their membership, and proceeded to hammer out a compromise piece of legislation. The long-term consequence of this tactical initiative was a precedent for cooperative efforts on the determination of legislative priorities taking into account all the major interests within the higher education community.

The collective presentation of policy positions had proved a durable one that has persisted to the discussions of preferred formulas for institutional aid in the early 1970s. The lessons of the disunity around the early federal aid discussions had such an impact on the higher education community that it tends to react with a degree of inflexibility on policy proposals that might loosen the existing bonds within the coalition. For example, the associations remained unified in their general preference for an aid formula proposed by Representative Edith Green, but in doing so exposed themselves to congressional charges that they had not given enough consideration to possible alternatives. One association spokesman agreed that the higher education community recognized the danger of becoming too committed to any particular formula, but wanted to present a united front in supporting any proposals. "All Congress has to hear is that we don't agree among ourselves," he said, "and it won't approve anything. That has happened in the past," he added, "and we don't dare get ourselves caught in that trap again." [10]

The desire to maintain unity within the higher education community has led a small minority of representatives to question the coalition on both philosophical and pragmatic grounds. Those challenging the assumptions of the coalition approach on philosophical grounds see efforts at consensus building as concealing rather than illuminating important and potentially critical questions about the relationship of higher education to government and to its own clientele, the students and institutions. In a fundamental sense, these objections represent a reaction to the emergence of the pragmatic perspective by those holding strong attachments to the more traditional view of higher education in politics. They regret that higher education seems increasingly willing to enmesh itself in adversary politics without thinking through their involvement and trying to justify its policy demands in the broader context of national priorities. These concerns are rarely confronted, and have been faced with decreasing frequency and sensitivity by a younger generation of politically aware representatives. These representatives see their role primarily in pragmatic terms of obtaining financial and program support for their institutions. They tend to have little regard for the overall effects of these policies on higher education. "Look," said one representative, "we haven't thought philosophically about higher education in the past twenty-five years. The money is being cut back now, the enrollments are leveling off, and we've had a general failure of the decision-making experience. The weakness of the administrations has been aggravated, the diffusion of power to the faculty has given way to the loss of thinking about higher education in general, to the rise of the pragmatic, self-interested approach. . . . The fact is that the fat years are gone, and we're starting on seven lean ones. And we're going to have to come up with some answers to these questions."

Another veteran representative anticipated that a primary source of conflict during the 1970s would be over the various proposals for federal aid to students and institutions. He was especially concerned about the lack of policy studies on the consequences of institutional grants over a number of years, and suggested that it should be feasible to explore the experience of the land-grant colleges to determine whether long-term federal financial support has made a discernible difference in the quality of these schools. The difficulty was that in trying to forge formulas based on extensive analysis of this sort they could potentially open up new areas of conflict and contention that would undermine the coalition approach.

A former ACE official felt that higher education did not dare to go back and reexamine the programs as they now existed. He was critical of higher education for endorsing the expenditure of federal funds for higher education without attempting to establish some priorities. He asserted that the American Council could "encompass anyone as long as the money was coming in," but defaulted in its obligation to assess the impact of various programs, particularly on undergraduates. The student protests and demonstrations simply pointed out that nearly all the support for programs was adopted without a clear assessment of their educational goals or values. Such assessments seemed to be done after the fact. Moreover, he added, the facade of unity in the Washington higher education establishment concealed the fact that certain groups had not received adequate representation of their own interests.[g]

The pragmatic response to the consensus approach has been to question whether each association is doing as well as part of the coalition as it would pursuing an independent effort. One observer commented that "some of the associations are beginning to ask whether they are losing more than they are gaining by presenting what they like to describe as a 'united front.' Some of your more aggressive associations like the junior colleges have in fact become more aggressive." [h]

A former federal relations officer for the junior college association explained that this impression of aggressiveness on the part of his membership was based not so much in the dollar amounts at stake in particular legislation, but the fear that other associations would be forced to pursue their own interests, thus creating divisiveness and contention within the higher education community.[i] His own feelings about the consensus approach were mixed.

---

[g] The question remains, however, about how much such calls for philosophical analysis can contribute to procrastination in the face of pressing political decisions by the Washington representatives. It seems that any effort to reassert the primacy of philosophical consideration would have the counterproductive effect of distracting attention from the immediate day-to-day political calculations of the representatives. The nature of philosophic analysis is bound to create debates and arguments that allow no durable conclusions, but that can take place only as continuing dialogues among the various interested parts of the higher education community. In a practical sense, such a shift would amount to a regression in the evolution of higher education as a national interest group.

[h] On several occasions the junior college association, the AACJC, allegedly acted contrary to the tacit community norms of the Washington establishment. For example, there has been an understanding that no association will actively protest legislation benefiting the institutional members of other associations. When the AACJC objected publicly to a bill drafted and enthusiastically endorsed by the AASCU and the NASULGC, several executive officers expressed their immediate disapproval to the offending AAJC officers. On several occasions the AACJC was alleged to have incurred the wrath of the Secretariat for offending the norm against campaigning too vigorously and independently in pursuit of special benefits for their own members. Harland G. Bloland, *Higher Education Associations in a Decentralized Education System* (Center for Research and Development in Higher Education, University of California, Berkeley, 1969), pp. 158–59.

[i] The American Council, as one of the primary molders of the unified coalition approach, has sought to sustain this tactical device. There exists within the American Council the attitude that the ACE is the mechanism through which the presidents of the constituent institutional members arrive at a consensus on policies involving government and higher education. More importantly, there is the feeling that the ACE should insist on being the only policy-stating agency in Washington for its constituents. While groupings of constituent members like the land-grant colleges are acknowledged as inevitable, it would be increasingly difficult for the ACE to sustain the close operating relationships it has with other associations. The uneasiness over the threatened proliferation of such groupings stems from anxieties about a resurgence of a pre-1960 situation where the efforts of the American Council would be vitiated by a myriad of voices claiming to speak for higher education.

I admit that there is a certain value to consensus just from the very nature of the decision-making process in Congress, where it seems far more fruitful to target on specific demands. But you have to remember that the consensus argument is one promoted by those in power rather than those out of power. With a small federal relations staff, the pressure for decisions on immediate questions such as wording of amendments, deletions, and inclusions, as well as on tactics and strategy, questions of judgment are always paramount. The situation tends to be one where a relatively few people have a fairly substantial amount of power. Consensus in this context simply means conceding a position; in other words, letting Jack Morse speak for you, allowing his own private style to take precedence.

The consensual approach is the tactical outcome of the pragmatic perspective. Because it has been associated with the legislative successes of the mid-1960s, certain representatives, particularly those in the American Council, have found it hard to keep in mind that the forging of consensus is a political tactic designed for specific instances and not a universal principle of policy-making success. The council, lacking clients with fairly homogeneous political demands, is virtually compelled to extol the virtues of unanimity and compromise, while other major associations represent common kinds of schools—colleges, land-grant universities, or junior colleges—with clear and distinctive interests. Hence, the question is not whether the higher education coalition is splitting apart, or functioning with increased harmony, but who stands to lose and who stands to benefit in specific instances. The Washington representatives would be negligent in their responsibilities to their own constituents if they did not weigh the gains and losses of cooperative lobbying as part of their political calculations, just as they would be remiss in their responsibilities if they were to jeopardize the opportunities for collective advantage by flagrant disregard for the coalition approach.[j]

The Activist Perspective

The traditional and pragmatic perspectives share the assumptions that higher education is a unique policy area deserving special recognition by

---

[j] Raymond A. Bauer, Ithiel de Sola Pool, and Lewis Anthony Dexter, *American Business and Public Policy* (New York: Atherton, 1963), p. 339, refers to efforts at achieving consensus on policy issues as "quasiunanimity," and concludes that "the broader and more heterogeneous the organization, the greater the probability that some subgroups will dissent on a given issue." Milbrath, in his study of the Washington lobbyists, noted that collaboration seemed to be most highly valued by organizations with large memberships—like farm and labor groups with considerable strength at the polls—and with professional staffs that work exclusively with Congress. He concludes that "collaboration is valued both by lobbyists and governmental decision-makers because it saves time and signifies the resolution of conflict. It is also clear, however, that collaboration is useful only in certain settings and that it is unwise where the conditions are not appropriate." Lester W. Milbrath, *The Washington Lobbyist* (Chicago: Rand McNally & Co., 1963), p. 174.

strategic elites, and that policy for higher education should be framed against the rational consideration of the broader national interest. The activist perspective, while it shares the assumption about the special quality of higher education, proceeds on the assumption that unique character no longer commands the automatic indulgence and support of the broader society. Instead, higher education stands in competition with other interests equally worthy of social support. In this view, political action becomes imperative if higher education's goals are to be realized. The most articulate statement of this position was by the former head of one of the state offices.

I feel that it's time we made an effort to bring national priorities into line with national interests and the national will. *Since politics involves the interplay of enlightened groups of self-interest, it is necessary to evolve ways to express these interests and since higher education is a clearly definable interest group, it is their responsibility to make clear the needs and interests of the education community, working through the existing system, and keeping up pressure in such a way as to bring national actions in accord with the national will,* for example, in the case of reduced spending for space and military projects. [Emphasis added.]

In effect, the activist view rejects the basic assumption of most higher education representatives about the rational determination of policy and replaces it with a perspective that sees policy as determined by the interaction of different interests operating on the basis of enlightened self-interest. In this context, not only does advanced learning retain its special character, but becomes an instrument used to redirect national priorities away from the hardware concerns of space exploration and military stockpiling to the humane concerns of health, education, and environmental protection.

Few of the representatives enthusiastic about a more activist role were quite so articulate. For the most part they laced their sentiments with strong doses of pragmatic political considerations. One representative from the office of a new, small association had no reservations about being involved with the full-funding effort.

Hell, everyone else does. Everybody else has been looking out for their interests, why shouldn't higher education? Sure, I'd be in favor of a permanent lobbying organization. Why shouldn't higher education have a lobby that looks out for its interests? Everyone else was seeking gain, and usually not in the public interest. Look at the aircraft, tobacco, and space interests. So why shouldn't higher education, especially when others are doing it for profit?

Another representative from a major association argued that higher education had been lax in pursuing its own interests, especially in the areas of funding and federal support. "You know," he said, "in some respects we're just like the Defense Department. We want more money." He argued, as did several of his colleagues, that the real significance of the Full-

Funding Committee was that it marked the first time that education had gotten together and held firm on a program serving their common interests. In doing so, it provided a precedent for future political activity. "I'd be in favor," he added, "of making the committee a permanent one because it would provide a single voice for all of education, rather than the multitude of individual spokesmen now running around the education field." (He did not explain how a coalition embracing all the interests in education would be any easier to maintain than a coalition made up solely of higher education representatives.) What is important, however, is the feeling that if higher education's interests are to be served, then it might be necessary to create different kinds of organizations and extend the coalition tactic beyond the confines of the higher education community.

Another official from a small association shared this sentiment about the Full-Funding Committee.

I was enthusiastic about it and I communicated my feelings to our membership. The coalition was certainly one mass of strange bedfellows, particularly since it included the impact aid people. But I didn't think this was a bad issue with which higher education should be linked, but instead saw it as a pragmatic instance of finding a good handle and then latching onto it. The Committee reflected a coming of age in terms of the realities of federal relations, even though I doubt that most of our college presidents would see it that way.

The executive secretary of one of the major associations summarized the perspectives on the Full-Funding Committee by pointing out that there were two main responses to it. The first seemed to say that higher education did not get much out of it, hence should go its own way. Furthermore, it probably lost some of its prestige by being associated with some of the hardware and audio-visual people, and the school superintendents. The other was manifested in the Washington offices of the AACJC and the AAC, who, in essence, argued that higher education had already lost whatever aura of prestige it might have had and hence had more to gain by a cooperative than independent effort.

I lean toward the latter view. There's probably more to gain by unity, and higher education already lacks good standing on the Hill in the wake of the student riots and demonstrations. There is some advantage in riding the coattails of a coalition that involved impact aid which has a powerful constituency on the Hill, even though certain tactics did upset people, particularly the strong-arm tactics attributed to the committee. For instance, there was a rumor that the NEA [National Education Association] threatened congressmen with defeat in the upcoming elections, but there's no way to verify it.

One representative felt that the Sullivan proposal had a good deal of merit because it avoided the inhibitions on political action by tax-exempt organizations. He added that many associations were increasingly hesitant about risking their tax-exempt status by becoming involved in lobby politics. He observed that there "probably would be a problem funding such an organization, but if the question were explored seriously, then it would be possible to implement it. It would at least have the advantage of working in the open until they could gain interpretations of the tax laws."

Another representative of a major association felt the Sullivan proposal was "an honest and open one" offered with the intention of insuring that higher education's interests were represented. "Frankly, I feel it is better to organize and register as a lobby rather than have the ACE, the AAC, and the other organizations maintain particular lobbying efforts of their own which tend to fragment and diffuse the potential impact of the united effort on the part of higher education." In addition, he thought the existence of such an organization would minimize the tax exemption question.

In spite of what several representatives saw as the advantages stemming from a separate lobbying organization, the Sullivan proposal was received somewhat less than enthusiastically by the major associations. The reasons for the cool reception perhaps rest in the interpretation given by a former ACE official. He commented that the Sullivan proposal was again in circulation at the Secretariat but had somehow slipped in through the back door.

If the fight is going to be so tough that on a pragmatic basis it will be necessary for higher education to get organized in a new way, and in a way which will minimize risks to their status. There is some potential in such a proposal and I'd like to see it studied. The upshot of such a study might be an organization composed as a formal lobby, while the associations would continue their own service functions. Keep in mind, though, that this is a threatening and disruptive kind of proposal, and if it were implemented, it would amount to a confession that the status quo was no longer adequate.

The activist perspective is held by a distinct minority within the major associations, and has slightly more support from the representatives in the small associations and state offices. It is still significant, however, because by minimizing the rational aspects of policy making and emphasizing the competitive, adversary nature of the political process, this view helps provide the ideological basis for a more assertive political role for higher education. Whether this adversary interpretation of national policy making is valid is not nearly as important for higher education as the fact that it provides a different way of looking at political action for the Washington representatives. Most representatives have been willing to accept the reconciliation of the traditional perspective with the pragmatic demands of their positions but for the most part have been unwilling to acknowledge the interplay of enlightened self-interest in politics. Instead, they see the contentiousness bred from the selfish pursuit of private goals.

More fundamentally, there seems to be a reluctance to concede that higher education has reached a point of social consequence in the knowledgeable society and is in fact a competitor along with a host of other more recent newcomers to the technological state like science and the giant corporation. In spite of the minority of representatives who cling to the traditional disdain for active political involvement and those advocating a far more aggressive political role for higher education, most of the Washington representatives find themselves in an intermediate position. They see what appears to be the inevitability of a shift toward a more assertive role, but they cannot go all out and endorse such a shift without agonizing over the deeply rooted assumptions about the style and demeanor of higher education in national politics. On the one hand, the full-funding experience was an adventure in tough politics for a small number of representatives and their constituents. For several it was an exhilarating experience. They revealed in pursuing goals they felt were above reproach as part of a team deeply engaged and committed to common objectives. The limited successes of the committee were appetizing enough to make the prospect of permanent organization a compelling possibility. On the other hand, there was an acute sensitivity to the fact that higher education was putting its self-perceived image and good will on the line by participating in bare-knuckled politics. The heart of this ambivalence rests in the feeling that, indeed, higher education's stakes have climbed tremendously over the past decade. But critical questions still remain about how best to consolidate gains already made, and how to promote the latest items on the policy agenda without throwing out a backlog of good will, prestige, and reputation for the accurate, thoughtful presentation of policy positions in a high-powered lobby effort. It is a position that is still struggling to balance the trade-offs between a more aggressive position and the potential gains and losses of taking on such a role.

The crucial tactic in this balancing effort is that of building and maintaining the ostensible policy consensus upon which the higher education coalition is premised. The experience of the early 1960s with the federal aid and church-state questions, and the ultimate legislative successes stemming from the political evolution of the coalition approach have become articles of faith among certain parts of the higher education community, particularly within the American Council. With no clearly homogeneous institutional constituency of its own, there is probably no better way for the council to mesh the different political interests of its constituents in order to present a coherent, relatively unified case to policy makers. One consequence of this tactic, however, is its bias toward limited change, the persistence of the existing distribution of power and prestige, plus a tendency to react to policy proposals rather than take the incentive for initiating new choices. In emphasizing the coalition tactic there are bound to be questions that do not get raised, let alone answered, issues that are bypassed, and interests that are inadequately represented—all in the name of higher education's unanimity. Whether this tactic or some other promises the best accommodation between the demands for political effectiveness and the style most compatible with the preferences of the Washington representatives remains one of the key questions in considering the emergence of higher education as a national interest group and its future political role.

Notes

1. Richard H. Sullivan, "Report of the president," *Liberal Education,* March 1969, pp. 137–48.

2. Ibid., pp. 142–43.

3. Ibid., p. 143.

4. Ibid., p. 144.

5. Robert M. Rosenzweig, paper in Seymout Harris, Kenneth Deitch, and Alan Levensohn, eds., *Challenge and Change in American Education* (McCutchan Publishing Corporation, 1965), p. 60.

6. Lawrence K. Pettit, "The Politics of Federal Policymaking for Higher Education," manuscript, chap. II, pp. 55–58.

7. Logan Wilson, "Perspectives on the American Council on Education," *Educational Record* 43 (January 1962): 18; emphasis added.

8. Homer D. Babbidge and Robert M. Rosenzweig, *The Federal Interest in Higher Education* (New York: McGraw Hill Book Company, 1962), p. 106.

9. Quoted ibid., p. 107.

10. Quoted in *Chronicle of Higher Education,* July 5, 1971.

5

The Associations Turn to Politics

The political bounds for the Washington higher education community were pretty well fixed by 1967. These were set by the continuation of political activism by two of the major associations, the National Association of State Universities and Land-Grant Colleges and the American Association of Community and Junior Colleges; the proliferation of vocal representatives from new state and small association offices; a growing number of representatives with political experience and a pragmatic attitude toward higher education's political role; and the consensus that the future prospects for academia were inextricably bound to federal policy. Three of the major associations, the Association of American Colleges (AAC), the Association of American Universities (AAU), and the American Council on Education (ACE), had only begun to adapt to the political changes that impinged more and more on their customary activities. These changes took two major forms, the first the mounting pressures from the membership for better grant-getting services, and the second, the proliferation of Washington representatives anxious to play a greater role in legislative relations.

Curiously, the emergence of private educational consultants exerted pressures on the institutional membership associations far out of proportion to their numbers, their influence, or their successes. Few association officials knew who these consultants were, who they claimed to represent, and what services they provided for their clients. But it seemed that increasing numbers of their own schools were turning to them. Naturally, association leaders felt compelled to initiate their own federal relations services. During the mid-1960s, for example, several AASCU colleges had turned to commercial firms to represent them (for what the association staff felt were outrageous rates) in federal grant-getting. To avoid the stigma of unresponsiveness to member needs, the AASCU leadership set up an Office of Federal Programs. Its main job was to get, process, and communicate information—and some occasional gossip—about pending or existing opportunities for federal support.

Pressures for improved membership services in grantsmanship were closely tied to the desire to have the Washington associations play a more aggressive role in political representation. These desires are reflected in the comments from two small association representatives. One cautioned that it was necessary to distinguish between legislative relations, which constituted lobbying, and federal relations, which did not. One reason for making this distinction, he continued, was that funds seemed to be drying up at the program level, so there was a growing interest in promoting legislation favorable to higher education.

As far as our own operation is concerned, I feel that eventually the federal relations aspects of maintaining and administering research funds should be shifted to on-campus people. It won't be long before they're nurtured enough so that the break can be made and the Washington office can dedicate itself more thoroughly to legislative affairs. Our new board seems to be more interested in constitutional questions and establishing closer contacts with the other associations and federal relations people, even though it doesn't seem to anticipate a greater amount of lobbying. They seem to feel that there should be a more active promotion in expressing their own interests.

The other representative explained that she had shifted her own attitude about playing a more active political role.

Two years ago I made a speech about what the Washington representative for higher education does. I emphasized the fact that I did not lobby, and that it was not my function as a Washington representative to lobby for these schools. Now, however, I feel that my concerns have shifted from the executive to the legislative branch. I'd like to spend more time at this end of my activities. If I did, though, I'd have to cut down on the services which I do provide to the faculties and administrations of our member colleges. I'm seriously limited in what I can do by the small size of my staff—there are just Sandy and I. I really did feel left out of the earlier hearings on higher education, and I really would like to keep closer contact with happenings on the Hill. Furthermore, I'm not content with what the associations have been doing in this respect and would prefer that they take more action on the legislative front.

These comments reflected a mood that was felt at different times and intensities within nearly all the major associations.

Association of American Colleges—Membership Pressure for Change

The Association of American Colleges (AAC) was one organization where these sentiments became translated into a membership uprising that forced the AAC into a far more explicit concern for political issues. These changes have been particularly significant because the AAC counted among its members some of the most vocal and adamant of any in higher education about the threats posed to academia by the federal government. Historically, the AAC schools took a distinctively conservative stance on the idea of a federal presence in higher education, motivated in part by ideological preferences for a limited federal role and in part by a desire to avoid potential conflicts over the church-state issue.

This rather staid political role took an abrupt turn during the spring and summer of 1967 when an insurgent group of college presidents came together to consider the problem of the independent liberal arts colleges' representation in policy making. That fall over 100 administrators from private four-year colleges and college associations met in Washington to determine how the independent liberal arts college could be most effectively represented to government and the public. A statement outlining the reason for the meeting noted that "the independent college finds itself increasingly fenced in as the imbalance between the private and public sectors of education becomes more pronounced. The national image and voice of private education is unclear and indistinct." [1]

Weimer K. Hicks, president of Kalamazoo College, and one of the organizers of the movement, observed that while the land-grant colleges had their spokesmen, as did the state colleges and universities, there was no group speaking solely for the independent colleges, especially the small private colleges. "Most of us connected with small colleges are anti-federal legislation," said Hicks. "We believe it is contrary to the concepts of the free enterprise system. But if the game is going to be played with Washington as the focal point then we have to be in Washington." He added that the AAC had been sympathetic to the problems of the small liberal arts colleges, but pointed out that it also represented a number of public institutions, and as a consequence, under its existing structure, the independent colleges had "no clear voice." [2]

This uprising was motivated by the growing sentiment among small college executives that their interests were taking a back seat to those of the public colleges and universities. Originally founded as a haven for the private liberal arts college, the AAC had evolved in a way that its main interests were generalized to all liberal education and not just the specific concerns of the small independent colleges. In making this shift the AAC had diffused its membership by adding a sizable number of deans from the liberal arts colleges of the large universities. The insurgents felt this shift had gutted the AAC's role as a lobby at a time when the large prestigious universities, the land-grant colleges, and the junior colleges had all established representation in Washington. The upshot was the distressing feeling that the small college of undergraduate education was the forgotten part of higher education.

Even though one AAC official stated that the association's position was one of "consistent support of small private institutions," he argued that it did not see itself as a "sectional or special interest group [but] as the champion of a special brand of general education. We are not organized to fight the land-grant boys or the state colleges." [3] He went on to say that if the insurgent group was merely expressing resentment about public institutions "taking an increasingly larger slice of the cake"—students, finances, etc.—there was no way of helping them by trying to reverse "this fact of life." If, however, they are talking about the problems involved in getting more and better faculty, students, and support, this, he said, "is a different question and one which we would like to help in ameliorating." [4]

The key goal of the private college movement, which became constituted as the Special Committee for Independent Colleges, was to alter the structure of representation rather than to determine policy. By the end of 1968 the AAC had committed itself to a major concern for the status of undergraduate institutions and had expanded its staff to include an expert to counsel member colleges in their search for federal grants. State organizations joined to found the Federation of State Associations in order to coordinate the efforts in behalf of the independent colleges on a national level. An AAC staff member was also added who was to devote full time as president of the Federation of State Associations and act as staff leader for the Commission on College and Society.

The effect the Special Committee had upon the structure and thinking of the AAC was dramatic for the speed with which the association responded, but more significantly for the challenges it posed to the overall structure of Washington representation. The Committee questioned the adequacy of existing federal relations activities and the place of the independent private college in the scheme of Washington representation. These issues simply had not been asked before this in-house revolt. The private colleges were successful for two reasons: first because of the zealous pursuit of clearly defined goals by their leadership; second because of the sympathetic reception it got from AAC president, Richard Sullivan. He was willing to go even further than the committee by calling for the creation of an independent organization, expertly staffed and well-funded, to act as the lobbying agent of higher education in Washington.[5]

The increasing openness of the AAC membership to proposals for more aggressive, assertive pursuit of their particular interests was indicated at the 1971 annual meeting where the Federation of State Associations of Independent Colleges and Universities announced its reorganization as the Council of Independent Colleges and Universities. Frederic W. Ness, president of the AAC, said the council would put together "a grass-roots support not previously available in like degree through any of our existing Washington associations." [6] At the same meeting, Howard R. Bowen, chancellor of the Claremont University Center, gave a blunt political speech in which he exhorted the AAC membership to go on the offensive in seeking financial aid for their institutions. He argued that private educators had to construct a "nationally agreed-upon program for government participation in the financing of private colleges and universities and . . .

work together to get this program adopted using every known device of public relations and political action." He argued the AAC to assume leadership in organizing the private colleges in a united effort to (1) "formulate a concrete and uncomplicated legislative program for both federal and state governments; (2) carry out a major national information program about private higher education; (3) mount a major political effort in Washington and in every state capital to bring about the enactment of needed legislation." [7]

Not only has the AAC been reoriented along more explicitly political lines and its particular interests brought largely in line with the other major associations, but on the practical working level it has also turned to a much more assertive form of representation. The kinds of options open to the Washington staff were reflected in a 1970 report on legislative activities and congressional outcomes. It noted that the staff had been faced with a range of possible tactics on numerous legislative issues, generally falling into three major categories:

Stimulation of action by other associations, followed by cooperation with them; cooperation with all concerned, and proceeding on our own (as with the amendments to the institutional grants bill). Obviously our resources do not permit full and independent action on all issues, even if this were desirable. In some cases potentially divisive action by us could even result in no gain for anyone. But we do stand ready to act independently where we feel the interests of a majority of members would be hurt were we to do otherwise.[8]

The transformation in the AAC's tone and posture toward political action is an impressive indication of the more general trend toward abandoning the aloof, almost condescending attitude toward politics that had pervaded much of higher education in earlier years. The change in the AAC is particularly significant for its member colleges were a major force in reiterating warnings about the perils of federal intervention as a consequence of federal aid. Pressing financial problems worked rapidly to erode this long and cherished ideological heritage. More significantly, the erosion of the traditional small college hostility toward a federal role helped clear away the ideological impediments to a more visible, aggressive role in interest representation.

Change at the Top: Association of American Universities

The transformation of the Association of American Universities (AAU) has been one of the more dramatic turnabouts in the Washington higher education community. For over half of its 75 year history the AAU acted as a standardizing and accrediting organization. For much of its recent history it has been the penultimate presidents' club.[9] The AAU presidents used to meet twice a year in closed sessions where deliberations were not made public and where explicit policy positions were rarely taken and publicized.

It was not until 1962 that the AAU opened its Washington office but even with this presence it remained content to let the American Council speak for its membership. The association had rarely taken stands on policy issues or offered testimony before congressional committees. One AAU spokesman explained the reason for this position.

There is a tendency in AAU to believe you can exhaust yourself by testifying too much. If you do speak out too much, you are not listened to. While some higher education associations take a position on everything, the AAU prefers not to exhaust its leverage by speaking out on too many issues.[10]

The massive upsurge of federal support for higher education and scientific research made such a passive role less and less tenable, particularly with the increasing number of claimants to federal dollars.

The AAU presidents devoted more and more time in the late 1960s to thrashing out possible directions for the association in federal relations. These deliberations came down to three essential alternatives: (1) maintain the position of the AAU as the model for educational quality; (2) perpetuate the AAU as a highly exclusive presidents' club; or (3) reconstitute the AAU as a political action committee. Several of the AAU presidents feared that an activist stance would add little to a situation where more and more interests were speaking out on educational questions. Others countered by arguing that the AAU should not remain silent on important issues or give to the American Council responsibility for representing AAU interests, especially since the ACE stance might in fact be at odds with positions taken by the AAU members.

By 1967 campus upheavals and the prospects for decreased federal support for higher education and university research became clear. Late that year at least one university president called explicitly for more sophisticated representation in Washington and asked his colleagues whether the public and private "high quality institutions" should band together to support a professional lobbyist in Washington. Such an individual would have had cabinet experience and be supported by a small staff. He felt there was serious doubt that existing organizations such as the ACE, and even the AAU, would be adequate to represent their interests. In addition, he raised the possibility of more effective use of member university trustees, reorganization of the Office of Education to be more receptive to the interests of higher education, improved representation of AAU interests by other associations, better contacts with Congress, and more effective use of alumni.

This candid exchange was significant. It reflected the clear recognition by the elite universities that status and prestige were no longer reliable political resources in a setting of increasingly organized and deliberate political activities by competing interests. There was a clear acknowledgment that Congress held the key to the policy-making process, as well as an explicit admission that in spite of the AAU's tradition of easy access to the executive branch, it would be in the legislature that most of the crucial battles would be fought. And it was precisely in the legislative branch that the AAU universities were least able to defend and promote their interests. In short, the AAU presidents were coming around to the view that there was a need for a vastly improved flow of ideas and information between Washington and the campuses as well as a need for a more activist political role.

Such a shift, however, involved two kinds of constraints, one the response of the other members of the higher education community, the other the response of their own more cautious colleagues. For example, in discussing the promotion of university interests, one president cautioned that no matter how much they stressed the commitment to quality in graduate education, they could not do this in a way that implied indifference to the problems of local and regional educational development. Instead, the universities had to stress how national institutions were an essential part of such development. They also realized that any contemplated political activities could not be especially blatant. One function of a specialized research operation would be to buttress policy positions with factual reporting and analysis.[a] As one member noted, universities might gain short-range advantages from a more aggressive lobbying approach, but their long-range interests and relations with government would be better served by a more apolitical stance and an atmosphere of objectivity.

The leadership of the AAU universities has been blessed with almost unlimited access to strategic elites in government, corporate, and foundation America. Early in 1968 representatives of 15 AAU schools (though ostensibly not meeting as members of the association) met at the New York headquarters of the Ford Foundation to continue their discussions about the nature of the Washington representation. Attending the meeting were National Science Board member Philip Handler, the Commissioner of Education, Harold Howe, and Ford Foundation chairman, Julius Stratton.

Though there was no argument about the value of such an office for coordinating research and compiling political intelligence, there was still

---

[a] Such an in-house policy and intelligence capability was not a front for academic charlatanism, or misrepresentation in such studies themselves. Rather, it reflects an appreciation for the way in which apparently factual material and analysis can be employed as a political resource. See, for example, Lauriston R. King and Philip H. Melanson, "Knowledge and Politics: Some Examples from the 1960's," *Public Policy*, Winter 1972.

considerable opposition to opening such an office. The reservations stemmed mainly from the ambivalent attitude of the university presidents toward political action. There was a fear that lobbying would arouse suspicions about higher education's intentions. Some also felt that there were competent and knowledgeable persons on campus who could ferret out more than could the staff of a Washington office and do a better job of research and analysis. In spite of these misgivings, there was a general feeling that the university presidents must be prepared to speak out more often and more concretely about the needs of higher education and especially about the needs of graduate education.

The sharpened impression that relations between the universities and the government were deteriorating, that the contraction of research funds was imminent, and that the persistence of campus turmoil had serious consequences for the graduate research universities compelled the AAU activists to make their move into federal relations during the fall of 1968. Their first goal was to identify an individual who could operate effectively in federal circles, who understood the federal policy-making machinery, and who was capable of dealing directly with his Washington counterparts in the other associations.

By early 1969 the AAU leadership formed the Council on Federal Relations and selected Dr. Charles V. Kidd as the director. Kidd had had extensive executive branch experience as the incumbent executive secretary for the Federal Council on Science and Technology, plus stints in the Social Security Administration, the Council of Economic Advisors, and the National Institutes of Health. Although most of his experience had been with executive branch politics, he had had continuing contact in a variety of positions with the federal support of university research and had written one of the pioneering books on those evolving relationships, *American Universities and Federal Research.*[11] In 1971 Kidd became the executive secretary of the association, thus initiating a new period of intensified political activity.

American Council on Education: Catching up with (Nearly) Everyone Else

Political change has come hard for the American Council. In spite of its extensive membership, relative wealth, and high visibility, it has yet to project a firm political identity within the Washington higher education community. Paradoxically, this size, prosperity, and visibility has resulted in an inertia that, when reinforced by the more traditional conservative attitudes about education's role in politics, has worked to inhibit the ACE's response to the political changes of the mid-1960s and early 1970s. According to a report reviewing the council's activities, "the role and goals of the ACE are unclear. Its program is too diffuse and lacks focus and purpose. Therefore, it remains a frequent source of concern and frustration to its constituents and to the offices of the Federal Government with which it works." [12]

The council was created as a confederation of 14 education associations in 1918 to unify higher education and forge consensus positions on issues linking higher education and government. At the fourth annual meeting of the Council in 1921, Director Samuel Capen complained about the planless, haphazard character of American higher education and the impossibility of unified action in the absence of a unifying agency. He saw in the formation of the American Council an end to that condition. "A unifying agency has now at last been established," he stated. "To stimulate discussion, to focus opinion, and in the end to bring about joint action on major matters of educational policy—these are the things that the American Council of Education was created to do. . . . This is the justification for the Council's existence, or there is none." [13]

In spite of this apparent enthusiasm for such a unifying organization, the council's prominence slipped appreciably during the interwar years. The ACE Federal Relations Commission was not set up until 1940. Even then it took nearly 30 years for this aspect of the council's activities to take firm shape.[b] In 1961 the council leadership prompted each of its member institutions to designate a campus representative to handle relations with the federal government. By 1963 there were over 500 institutional representatives with direct ties to the council's Washington office. The federal relations staff was also bolstered from one part-timer to five full-time specialists, and a monthly newsletter (*Higher Education and National Affairs*), a manual of federal programs bearing on higher education, and a teletype service for quick contacts with council members were established.

As a result of several reorganizations that became fully effective in 1962, the balance of power in the organization shifted from the constituent associations to the institutional members. The change was reflected most significantly in the creation of a board of directors made up of prestigious university executives who boosted the national stature of the council and the expansion of the membership base in a way that helped shore up the

---

[b] The American Council did not assume a central role as a spokesman for higher education until late in World War II. One historian found that "prior to America's entry into World War II, the voice of the American Council on Education in the councils of the federal government was weak and in certain circles barely audible. Presidents of the United States seldom sought its advice. Cabinet officers sought it only infrequently. Congressmen often drafted legislation affecting the colleges and universities without consulting ACE." William M. Tuttle, Jr., "Higher Education and the Federal Government: The Lean Years, 1940–42," *The Record—Teachers College*, December 1969, p. 267; and "Higher Education and the Federal Government: The Triumph, 1942–1945," ibid., February 1970, pp. 485–99.

council's financial base. The reorganization, however, was not a boost to the council's skills or determination to move aggressively as the political vanguard for the community. In fact, the council's conservative style, its general lack of responsiveness to marginal members of the postsecondary community, and its reluctance to play a more assertive political role, combined to inhibit any major changes in the direction of more overt political activities.

The traditional perspective on the unique place of higher learning (as described in Chapter 4) was one of the most characteristic features of the council under the leadership of Logan Wilson. Wilson's organizational model was the traditional liberal arts university, not the trade association. Prestige, hierarchy, and status were more important to the council leadership than accommodation, diplomacy, access, and co-optation. The style that resulted from these values was characterized by a former council official as "stodgy, conservative, even a bit on the dour side." Another representative, trying to capture the tone set by the council leadership, finally exclaimed that "if the American Council staff were running a university, it would probably look like Grayson Kirk's Columbia." One former ACE officer was far more pointed in his assessment of the council. "Probably the worst aspects of higher education are reflected in the American Council," he said. "We represent the worst in academic conservatism, elitism, and concern for prestige and the status quo."

One consequence of this conservative attitude and style has been an identification of the ACE as the instrument of the most prestigious schools in the country, and particularly of the presidents and top administrators of these schools. Logan Wilson candidly admitted that the council exists mainly for the benefit of college administrators. In spite of the 1962 reorganization, the council had "continued primarily as a service organization, with its focus on policy questions, chiefly those of significance to professional decision-makers—the principal officers of academic administration." He went on to state that the council's coordinating function was inherent in the representative character of its board, commissions, and committees, and in their deliberations and actions. In its federal relations role, he asserted that the ACE had "come to be the principal national spokesman for higher education and the primary source of information to institutions on Federal programs and policies. This role relates closely to its functions of interpreting to educators the issues involved in governmental policies and of helping higher education develop national policies." [14]

Generally, this attitude has been translated into an emphasis on the concerns of universities and colleges that have elitist traditions, strong research investments, and the firmest contacts with Congress and the executive. It has tended to exclude other claimants, particularly the predominantly black colleges, junior colleges, and students. The prevailing assumption has been that college presidents are the only people concerned with the problems of colleges and universities as complete institutions. One former ACE official pointed out that the consequence of this self-conscious alignment with college administrators was to place itself "consistently (and by its own lights, 'naturally') in an adversary position with fair frequency in relation to students, faculty, nonprofessional staff members, and the larger community." For example, during the legislative fight over the 1972 Higher Education Amendments higher education representatives, working mainly through the council, were sharply criticized by some senators, representatives, and their staffs for pursuing institutional operating support and devoting little energy to lobbying for student-aid needs.[c]

These biases toward established institutions and their executives were reinforced by an attitude that was openly distrustful of individuals outside the normal circle of traditionally distinguished institutions. A council executive elaborated on this attitude by explaining that

it's very difficult to include certain associations and representatives because we don't know them that well and we don't dare to just open it up to a lottery system of commission representation because we simply would be unsure about the caliber of membership. There is a high concentration of high caliber people on the commission and various staff positions because they are people of good reputations, people that we know, either through other members or through their own personal contacts.

These biases have also colored the ACE view of the two-year colleges. By its own admission one of the most perplexing dilemmas faced by the council has been how to treat the junior colleges. One ACE official who was regularly involved in representing the political interests of higher education felt that one of the hardest parts of his work was finding the proper relationship for the two-year colleges in the framework of higher education. He was frustrated because he did not feel these schools knew themselves whether they wanted to stress the vocational and training programs that grew out of secondary education, or strive to become full-fledged institutions of higher learning. He complained about their view that they came out on the short end of federal programs because it was "hard for me to see their point of view. What they do is to mass all the federal education programs and then calculate their share on that basis, rather than on how

---

[c] *Chronicle of Higher Education,* July 3, 1972. In another instance, the council responded to the increased campus political activities associated with the congressional campaigns of 1970, by warning that schools that inadvertently involved themselves in political campaigns ran the risk of losing their tax exemption. To minimize this risk the council issued guidelines on campus facilities, schedules, and solicitation practices that were approved by the Internal Revenue Service. *New York Times,* November 9, 1970. This is simply another illustration of the council's tendency to come down clearly on the side of the status quo represented by campus administrators.

much they derive from specific programs. For example, most of the federal money has gone to large science programs and it's extremely difficult to relate the existence of a large science program to junior colleges, even though this may be an instance of adding apples or oranges."

Another ACE official admitted candidly that "the ACE has never accepted an obligation to assess the needs of or to really represent junior colleges or community colleges. I am not saying it should have, though I will point out that in a few short years they will have far more political muscle than ACE. Unless and until it does, ACE cannot object to the presence in Washington of an association of junior colleges which makes its own policies and has already demonstrated its ability to sell its approach to the Congress."

Another consequence of this style and attitude was an inflexible, and often ill-tempered reaction to challenges or criticisms, particularly those originating outside the confines of One Dupont Circle. For example, shortly after President Nixon had delivered his 1970 higher education message, eight AAU presidents met with the president to express their concern about the policies implied by the message. The AAU contingent sought a hearing with the president as representatives of the AAU, and not from the American Council, which claimed to be the spokesman for higher education in Washington. A top ACE official responded rather irritably when asked about this event. He was quick to assert that the AAU did not have any more access than did the ACE. The AAU, he continued, had invited presidential counselor Daniel Moynihan to speak with them about the education program. In the wake of their questions and objections to the administration's program, Moynihan checked with the president who agreed to see a select number of AAU presidents. "This is the way that they got to see the President," he said. "We could meet with the president just about whenever we wanted to, but we simply haven't had occasion to yet."

This sensitivity to criticism also led to an embarrassing display during the spring of 1971 when the Secretariat, the informal group of 14 association executives, was requested by then secretary of the Department of Health, Education, and Welfare, Elliot L. Richardson, to comment on the Newman Committee Report on Higher Education. The critique, transmitted to Richardson under Logan Wilson's signature, attacked the Newman effort as a " 'non-report'—too long and pejorative as a briefing memo, too short as a scholarly examination;" that restated familiar criticisms; was "replete with internal contradictions;" and ignored "the existence of a vast number of recommendations that respond specifically and directly to the issues it raises."

The higher education establishment, represented quintessentially by the American Council, perceived the report as doing only more damage to the public image of the academy. "It is a damaging report to the extent that . . . it creates scapegoats. Its dissemination—already begun—will intensify the antagonism of opinion leaders and legislators who are already suspicious of higher education. Some prominent educators have already indicated their judgement that it will erode support for higher education." [15] This strident, defensive response reflected a leadership that had grown complacent in a period of good-will toward education, and petulant and inflexible in responding to even the mildest.recommendations for change.

The basis for these attitudes is not hard to pinpoint. They formed at a time when the links between the national government and higher education were tenuous at best. Policy statements tended to be expressed in general terms. There were no widespread campus disruptions and demonstrations to call public attention to conflicts within higher education. Colleges and universities did in fact hold a prominent place in the scheme of national values, largely as a result of both the prestige of the universities and their leadership and the unchallenged relationship between higher education and occupational success. Politically, there were few government programs that benefited certain colleges and universities and not others in ways that set different institutions against one another.

The third big area of dissatisfaction with the council is in the conduct of the higher education community's political business. It has been regularly disparaged for its tendency to react to policy initiatives rather than generate them; to provide inadequate data on policy issues too late in discussions; to focus its efforts on a few legislators rather than at strategic points in both the executive and legislative branches; and for the diffuse federal relations structures that confused and frustrated legislators seeking help and guidance on policy issues.

These political deficiencies became painfully apparent during the fight over the 1972 Higher Education Amendments. The associations pursued, as they had in the past, a close working relationship with Oregon's Democratic congresswoman, Edith Green, in trying to draft an acceptable institutional aid bill. The major interest of the associations in general institutional support made an alliance with Mrs. Green a logical step. The key spokesmen for the associations, Jack Morse of the American Council and Ralph Huitt of the Land-grant Association, together with their colleagues at One Dupont Circle managed to hammer out a consensus formula based on student enrollments and level of education. Their general sentiment was that this was the best approach because it was simple, easy to understand, and avoided the potentially explosive issue of allocating funds according to somewhat subjective assessments of "need."

Once they had agreed to rally behind Mrs. Green's leadership in pressing her slightly modified version of the institutional support plan, the educators became inflexible in their commitment to both Mrs. Green and the formula. On the basis of their prior close contacts with her, her skills as a legislator, and reputation as a champion of higher education, it made perfectly good sense for the educators to back her. What they could not foresee were the twists of fortune and personal conflicts that sapped her effectiveness to the point where she lost control over the fate of the legislation.

Equally unfortunate was the tendency for the representatives to revert to their predictable political bad habits. Once they had stated their policy preference and endorsed the efforts of Mrs. Green on their behalf, they simply backed off to watch the legislative pulling and hauling in the House and Senate. There was no sustained effort by the educators to perform missionary work among other legislators, particularly the Senate, or in providing useful data and information to support their case. The most frequent criticism levied by congressional staffers and their bosses was that the educators relied too much on Mrs. Green to defend their positions and neglected to keep good lines of communication open to other lawmakers on the Senate and House education subcommittees. Rhode Island Democrat Claiborne Pell, who ended up playing a pivotal role in designing the final legislation and its emphasis on student aid, complained that "I need help, and I haven't gotten a damn thing from the ACE." [16] In short, the 1972 experience brought home forcefully the need for the higher education community to expand and to cultivate support wherever it could find it; buttress its policy positions with credible, carefully-wrought documentation; and follow through statements of preferred policy positions with regular contacts with federal policy makers.

In spite of the Council's self-proclaimed role as the chief spokesman and coordinator for the higher education community, the amount of resources devoted to these activities provide one reason for the problems described above. In 1973, for example, out of an overall budget of some $4 million, only about $150,000 went to support the federal relations staff.[17] This staff has been particularly well-suited to grapple with the technical details of legislation. One staff member handles the tedious intelligence-gathering aspects of the office by reading through the *Congressional Record,* agency releases, and other information services to cull items of interest to the membership. An attorney who is a specialist in tax law deals with the technical implications of legislation, and until his retirement in 1974, John (Jack) Morse, the federal relations director, handled contacts with legislative and executive decision makers. He had been the individual to whom legislators turned most frequently when they wanted information about higher education's reaction to proposed legislation or additional data to assist them in evaluating new policies.

The critical turnabout for the ACE came with the retirement of Logan Wilson and his succession in January 1972 by Roger Heyns, former chancellor of the University of California, Berkeley. About a year later Heyns announced the appointment of Stephen K. Bailey as council vice-president, thus filling a job that had been vacant for over two years. Bailey, a prominent political scientist from the Policy Institute of the Syracuse University Research Center, was recruited to assist Heyns and to direct the council's federal relations program.

This change in top leadership was critical for setting a new direction for the council. Their first concrete step was to concede the validity of the charges levied at the council and acknowledge that the tone, style, and skills of the old council were no longer appropriate for the egalitarian revolution that had overtaken higher education. Bailey, in the keynote address at the ACE's 1973 annual meeting observed that, "Today we scarcely know who we are, let alone who's in charge. We no longer are 'higher,' we are simply—or perhaps less grandly—post-secondary." By indirection, he also chided his colleagues for their pretensions at a time when many of the affectations peculiar to university administrators looked rather foolish to those more and more concerned about what they were getting from their higher education dollar. "To top it all off," he said, "we exist in this ambiguous and dangerous jungle doubting that we are armed with the skills and attitudes appropriate to survival. Whether we believe it to be fair or just, we have a reputation—at least in this town—for being exclusive, self-indulgent, patronizing and sloppy. In an increasingly egalitarian world, our own generally accepted, if slightly droll, status displacements (from Harvard to Cornell to Syracuse to Oswego State to Onondaga Community College to Ajax Business School) are no longer amusing." [18]

Under Heyns' leadership the council has gradually opened up to members who in the past lingered in the shadows of the elite universities. The changing composition of the board of directors is one example. Under the Wilson council the members of the board were the executive officers of institutions and higher education systems. During 1969–70, for example, all but two of the 22 positions were filled by college and university presidents, including the presidents or chancellors of Yale, Stanford, Berkeley, Johns Hopkins, Notre Dame, and Amherst. A 1973 constitutional change expanded the board to include six representatives from member associations, thus redressing a long-standing complaint of the associations during the Wilson administration.[d] At the same time, the board has become more broadly representative of the higher education community. In addition to

---

[d] Several associations tried to gain a larger role in the council's policy-making activities in 1968 but to little avail. See *Chronicle of Higher Education,* April 8, 1968. A significantly expanded role for the associations was also a major recommendation of two detailed studies of the council and its place in the higher education community. See, Harland G. Bloland and O. Meredith Wilson, "Report on the Higher Education Secretariat Community, Washington, D.C.," August 1971, photocopy; and John C. Honey and John C. Crowley, "The Future of the American Council on Education—A Report on Its Governmental and Related Activities," September 1972, photocopy.

the six elected association members, for example, the 1973–74 board was made up of members from two-year schools, small liberal arts colleges such as Rollins, Scripps, Wellesley, and Mundelein, and schools not usually ranked high on the prestige ladder, such as Jackson State University and the University of Wisconsin, Green Bay.

Heyns was also candid in acknowledging that the council could justifiably be criticized for its failure to get useful information to policy makers in timely fashion. He went on to summarize the deficiencies of the council in this area.

We have tended to get into policy discussion too late in the process, often at the stage when particular pieces of legislation have already been introduced. We have paid too little attention, relatively speaking, to departments other than HEW within the executive branch, both with respect to the development of policy and the implementation of legislation. We present too diffuse a structure for legislators or executives to know where to turn for help. Our consultative mechanisms are by and large informal, and as a result information exchange is often imperfect and we lose important and useful contributions. As a second consequence of this informality, we legitimately incur the criticism that we leave people out of the process who ought to be included.[19]

This sweeping summation of what had been troubling the council's detractors was the necessary first step in turning the council around. In the all-important area of federal relations the signs through 1974 were sometimes contradictory but a general direction was beginning to take shape. Heyns stated his intention to bolster the federal relations activities of the council by increasing the staff and budget and by increasing its scope to work more with the executive branch, state governments, and provide better statistical information for decision makers.[20] Bailey's appointment was a big step in this move beyond the council's historical fixation on the Congress to an explicit concern for the executive branch.

Although the idea of a policy analysis capability within the education community had been around for quite some time,[e] it took the jolt of the 1972 amendments fight and a change in the top leadership of the council to get such a service underway. In August 1973 the council set up a Policy Analysis Service (PAS) to assist the council in presenting policy issues and responding to information requests from the Congress and Executive. The

---

[e] Sullivan's proposal and the creation of the Council on Federal Relations by the AAU were two examples. A 1971 study of the Secretariat noted that "study and analysis of the consequences of executive, legislative and judicial action, as well as of proposed legislation, would buttress the ACE's own policy positions in the federal relations sphere, and, if results were widely disseminated to constituent associations, would provide them with a valuable resource which they themselves are unable to duplicate." Bloland and Wilson, "Report on the Higher Education Secretariat," p. 4. Had their advice been heeded, the educators might have avoided the debacle over the 1972 Amendments.

10-member staff conducts analyses or studies of specific policy issues such as student and institutional support, affirmative action, or long-range manpower estimates. It also puts together brief summaries of policy issues and compiles factual data bearing on important issues that are of value to other activities sponsored by the council. The PAS has also provided a vehicle for improving contacts with government decision makers by convening seminars on topics of mutual concern.

The PAS is clearly designed to perform a staff function within the council, and though it serves under the general leadership of Vice-President Bailey, it does not act as an arm of the Office of Federal Relations except insofar as it provides specific services to that office.

In the overall context of the ACE organization, these modest shifts toward broader representation and enlarged and more directed staff work in federal relations do not signal a major effort to redirect the council to a more activist political role. The best indication that such changes are not likely is reflected in the response to a recent study on the council's place in the higher education community and its role in federal relations.[21] The report, commissioned by Roger Heyns as a report to the president of the council, was based on extensive interviews with association and government officials, and other observers of the higher education community. It turned up the familiar litany of complaints about elite domination, unrepresentative and unresponsive leadership and general ineffectiveness in policy making. These deficiencies were attributed to a failure of council leadership which was seen as "basically aloof, excessively devoted to scholarly research and publications and to a variety of other specific programs which are largely unrelated to its leadership function." [22]

The remedy for these ills was a drastic reorganization that was to reorient the council towards political activism. Programs peripheral to these political activities were to be sheared off; the council was to reorganize as a confederation of associations representing all the major constituencies in higher education (including those normally considered outside the ACE orbit), and staff up to become the chief spokesman for higher education. The presidency was to be strengthened and the board made more representative. A key part of the revamped council was to be an expanded Office of Governmental Affairs that was to compile political intelligence; develop close liaison with Congress; help the council president and board chairman prepare and present policy positions; develop formal and informal contacts within the executive branch; and analyze pending legislation. In addition, an Office of Political Development was to act as the political education arm of the ACE. Funding for these efforts would become available once the Office of Research, the Program Development Office, the Commission on Academic Affairs, and the Commission on Administrative Affairs were put out of business.

Given these radical prescriptions, it was hardly surprising that Heyns did not embrace the report in its entirety. Although a number of steps have been taken that are compatible with the recommendations of the report (recruitment of a vice-president [Bailey] primarily responsible for federal relations, expanded association representation on the board; creation of the Policy Analysis Service; and removal of the Office of Research to the Berkeley campus) Heyns openly rejected most of the other recommendations. He stated that he would "not recommend that the Council be exclusively (or nearly so) concerned with governmental relations." [23]

In short, the council may appear to be a bit less exclusive, a little more open to those earlier considered at the fringes of the higher education establishment, and organized a bit more deliberately to provide political intelligence through mechanisms like the Policy Analysis Service. In the context of the changes that took place during the late 1960s, however, the ACE is simply playing catch-up. It has again reacted to events and pressures external to it, and has not been at the forefront of the community in creating new institutions or energizing old ones. But this consolidating role may in fact be the most appropriate one for the council to play, a role that the Heyns' administration is trying to assume with some degree of self-consciousness.

The council is an easy target if it is judged by political criteria alone. Invariably its performance and behavior is set against that of the more experienced and visible interest groups like agriculture, business, industry, and labor. The Honey-Crowley report, for example, deliberately concentrated on the ACE's performance in governmental relations to the exclusion of the council's service roles. The recommendations were clearly inspired by the organization and tactical performance of more experienced interest groups. It provided a blueprint for political action with emphasis on organization, political intelligence, and policy research. Although not directly concerned with the council, the Sullivan proposal was also inspired by this model.

The model, however, does not provide a rigid framework for what constitutes an effective political organization. Effectiveness cannot be measured solely in terms of legislative victories, but must also be judged according to the capacity of an organization to enlist the support and enthusiasm of its membership. The council's primary sustenance is the range of services and amenities it provides, the symbolic role it plays as the largest and most visible of the higher education organizations, and its historical role as the organization to which government officials turn on matters relating to higher education. The council provides visibility and continuity, a touchstone for the collective identity of the higher education community. To those caught up in the day-to-day politicking in and around the associations, these sources of ACE strength may not look very impressive. To the college president or dean, the council and its activities looks quite different.[f] Moreover, provision of programs and services like the offices of Academic Affairs, Women in Higher Education, Administrative Affairs and Educational Statistics, and Leadership Development in Higher Education results in external constituencies and internal pockets of entrenched interests that become hard to eliminate.

And it is this sensitivity to the distinction between the role the council can play for its diverse membership that distinguishes Heyns from his successor. Lacking the rigid commitment to the traditional ideology about higher education and government, Heyns has indicated a good sense of what is at least politically *feasible* for the council. Specifically, he has recognized the constraints imposed by the diversity of the membership, the territorial instincts of the other associations, and the overriding consideration that all the associations are voluntary, just as cooperation among the associations is voluntary.[24]

In this kind of setting he has realized and stated explicitly that the council should be a coordinator and not an activist. "We're not trying to get to be a big empire," he said. "What we're trying to do is see where capabilities lie and then help those activities rather than duplicate them. Unless it's a gap nobody else can fill, we're not going to fill it." [25]

One way Heyns hopes to put this approach to the community division of labor is "the concept of the chosen instrument," in which there would be collective agreement that an agreed-upon function would be the particular responsibility of a given association. In such a case, there would be an understanding that no one else would try to duplicate the activity and that all would help the "chosen instrument." [26]

Heyns' comments are significant in the context of the Washington associations because they marked a public disavowal of the council's earlier implicit—and often explicit—claims to speak and act on behalf of all higher education. To be sure, the ACE was more or less forced into this position. And Heyns' invocation of the "chosen instrument" was in some respects a recognition of the existing situation and not a new policy design. When Logan Wilson's administration failed to respond to issues such as faculty collective bargaining, and women's rights, other organizations

---

[f] It is interesting to note that in spite of the persistent gripes about the council, dropping out of the ACE was mentioned by only one representative, an officer of one of the student associations. When asked about his impression of the American Council, he smirked and commented that "ACE is nothing but a bunch of old bureaucrats representing the administrators and making studies about how they can run their institutions. I can't think of one thing they've done for higher education in America, despite the amount of money they haul in. They're political as hell. . . . The only reason we're still in it is to get the crap they send out, their newsletter on legislation, which I don't have time to keep track of myself. I suppose it's almost a subversive kind of membership, because we do like to keep some tabs on what they're doing."

moved in and are predictably reluctant to surrender their initiatives back to the Council. Nonetheless, the self-conscious effort to accommodate to these changes gracefully, and perhaps even effectively, bares witness to a new openness on the part of the council leadership to some new realities in the Washington political environment.

Finally, the council is limited in how far it can move out in front of its member associations. Again, the relations between the associations are voluntary. The leadership of the council has few sanctions it can use to keep their colleagues in line. Conversely, the officials of the other associations may be given to firing off broadsides at the council, but the fact remains that it is hardly in their own interests to automatically subordinate their political judgements and activities to the ACE. In such a setting openness of communication and diplomatic skills become paramount.

One mechanism for trying to mesh this coordinating role with the voluntary nature of the community was the creation of what became known as the Higher Education Secretariat. Shortly after the 1962 reorganization representatives from the major associations argued that the ACE had defaulted on its stated responsibilities to coordinate the activities of its members and urged that the ACE hold regular meetings of the executive secretaries of these associations. The 14-member group, meeting informally with no formal agenda and no votes, seeks consensus on the basis of discussions rather than threats or sanctions.[g] Although these meetings have helped preserve intimacy, close contact, and candid exchanges within the higher education establishment, most members have not viewed the Secretariat as an action group. One association president explained that "It's not a group with form or structure; just a once-a-month meeting where no action on behalf of the Secretariat really takes place. I really prefer to go to the Rotary Club and talk to somebody outside this area on occasion."

Another Heyns innovation to get around the limits of the Secretariat has been to bring together the elected heads and the chief executives of the five major institutional-membership associations (AASCU, NASULGC, AAU, AAC, and AACJC) to constitute themselves as a coordinating committee within the council. These associations, representing some 95 per cent of all institutions, are to act as an informal advisory committee to Heyns in carrying out the ACE's role as coordinator. Specifically, the committee

---

[g] The members in 1974 were American Association of University Professors; National Commission on Accrediting; Association of Governing Boards of Universities and Colleges; American Association of Community and Junior Colleges; National Association of State Universities and Land-Grant Colleges; Association of American Universities; National Catholic Educational Association; Association of American Colleges; American Association of State Colleges and Universities; Council of Graduate Schools in the U.S.; American Association of Colleges for Teacher Education; American Association for Higher Education; Council for the Advancement of Small Colleges; American Council on Education.

is to facilitate interassociation cooperation; assist in defining respective roles and carving out joint responsibilities; and exchange information and seek ways to cut down on duplication of effort.[27]

The transition from Wilson to Heyns in 1972 marked the ascendency of the pragmatic over the traditional perspective within the council. Heyns and Bailey were explicit in repudiating the tenor and style that became the public expression of the traditional ideology. In doing so they cleared the way to making the council more open to its membership, more deliberate in its federal relations activities and less arrogant, in proclaiming its primacy as the principle spokesman for higher education in Washington. That this ascendency took as long as it did is testimony to the durability of the traditional perspective under the Wilson administration. Unfortunately, a view of the proper relationship of higher education to government and the relationship of various institutions to one another which was fitting and reasonable at the beginning of the 1960s had grown stale, dogmatic and reactionary when challenged by the turmoil during the latter part of that decade.

Equally important the very diversity of interests embraced by the council had the paradoxical effect of diffusing protests about the way the ACE conducted its business. There were simply no readily identifiable interests within the council that could act as catalysts for change. A comparison of the ways these changes came to the AAU and AAC is illuminating as a contrast to the ACE experience. For both the AAU and the AAC there was a clear and painful recognition of the impending financial plight of the colleges and universities. It was also apparent that the federal government was already playing, and would continue to play, a key role in supporting higher education. The response to these readings of the political setting was markedly similar in both cases. A persuasive minority was able to promote significant changes in the traditional forms of association representation, in the case of the AAC by creating a structure within the organization for the explicit use of the private colleges, and in the case of the AAU, establishment of a brand-new federal relations staff and office grafted onto the older association.

At this point, however, there are some important contrasts. The AAU schools were increasingly sensitive to their collective images amidst the student disruptions and felt the prestige that had sustained them as a presidents' club in the past slipping away. The private liberal arts colleges, however, were concerned about getting a Washington voice where they felt there was none working specifically on their behalf. Once the decision was made for the universities, the nature of the federal relations operation was drafted with deliberate precision and staffed by a man judged most capable on the basis of prior experience and reputation for carrying out the work of the Council on Federal Relations. In contrast, the AAC had a much larger and more diverse constituency which made this kind of planning and precision difficult to carry out. Moreover, there were repeated pressures for expanding the service aspect of the AAC federal relations operation to assist member schools in grant work and participation in federal programs.

Pressures on the ACE were never so well-defined or clearly expressed by identifiable groups within the organization. Instead there was a pervasive undertone of dissatisfaction over what was seen as the unrepresentative and unresponsive nature of the council and its leadership by those looking to the council to play a more active political role. Along with this undertone were external pressures for change that reinforced the cases made by advocates of change within the associations. Many of these pressures came from the growing number of small associations and individual college offices spreading throughout the community. Representatives from these offices have been especially well-equipped to force change on the major associations because it is much easier for them to achieve some sense of unanimity because of their fairly homogeneous membership. Because they are typically staffed by just one man or woman they have substantial leeway to set policy for the membership.

In contrast the big associations have diverse constituencies and fairly regular procedures for reaching collective policy decisions. They lack the kind of laissez faire style that is particularly suitable for the small offices. Moreover, once a policy position is reached the association, as the public representative of a clearly defined membership, must take on the responsibility for implementing any such decisions, a responsibility that the small offices are not able to accept. The ACE leadership felt that the spread of the small offices and associations represented a clear threat to ACE's self-ascribed hegemony in political affairs, and specifically that this proliferation would make it increasingly difficult to maintain close relationships with other associations and representatives. In short, the small associations, in spite of their limited clienteles, resources, and institutional prestige, still have had the capacity to press certain kinds of action on the large associations that by their nature and composition are inherently slow in seizing initiatives and staking out new areas of service or political activity.

Still, it would be misleading to attribute to these associations a more important role than they deserve. Though they were significant in alerting the leadership of the associations to the growing sentiment in favor of a more clearly defined political role for higher education, the fact remains that the leadership had to assess the meaning of these developments and act upon them. In retrospect, the single most important cause in the associations' turn to politics was the openness and receptivity of the leadership to the complaints of their memberships. The one glaring example where this did not take place at a pace comparable to that sweeping through the rest of the community was the American Council under Logan Wilson.

Change in the council, however modest, still had to wait for the transition in leadership and the catharsis of public confession before getting on with the business of equipping the organization to improve its political effectiveness. Having come this far, however, raises the additional questions about the prospects for future changes in the higher education community. These prospects are the concern of the next chapter.

Notes

1. Quoted in *Chronicle of Higher Education,* October 12, 1967.

2. Ibid.

3. Ibid.

4. Ibid.

5. Richard H. Sullivan, "Report of the President," *Liberal Education,* March, 1969, pp. 137–48. His proposal is discussed in Chapter 4.

6. Quoted in *Chronicle of Higher Education,* January 18, 1971.

7. Ibid.

8. "Legislative Activity and Congressional Outcomes," *Liberal Education,* March, 1970, pp. 118–19.

9. William K. Selden, "The AAU—Higher Education's Enigma," *Saturday Review,* March 19, 1966, pp. 76–78, sketches the history of the AAU.

10. Quoted in Harland G. Bloland, *Higher Education Associations in a Decentralized Education System* (Center for Research and Development in Higher Education, University of California, Berkeley, 1969).

11. Cambridge: Belknap Press, 1969.

12. John C. Honey and John C. Crowley, "The Future of the American Council on Education—A Report on its Governmental and Related Activities," September 1972, photocopy, p. 4.

13. Charles G. Dobbins, ed., *American Council on Education and Leadership and Chronology 1918–1968* (American Council on Education, Washington, D.C.: 1968), pp. 7–8.

14. Logan Wilson, "The Council Since 1961," in Dobbins, ed., *Leadership and Chronology,* p. 157. For one critical view of the council, see Paul Lauter and Archibald W. Alexander, "ACE: Defender of the Educational Faith," *The antioch Review* 29 (Fall 1969): 287–303.

15. "Critique of Newsman Report," Transmitted by Logan Wilson to Hon. Elliot Richardson, April 17, 1971, photocopy.

16. Quoted in *Chronicle of Higher Education,* October 30, 1972.

17. *Chronicle of Higher Education,* October 30, 1972.

18. October 11, 1973, photocopy, available from the American Council on Education.

19. Roger W. Heyns, "The National Educational Establishment: Its Impact on Federal Programs and Institutional Policies," *Liberal Education,* May 1973, p. 156.

20. *Chronicle of Higher Education,* October 30, 1972.

21. John C. Honey and John C. Crowley, "The Future of the American Council on Education—A Report on Its Governmental and Related Activities," September 1972, photocopy.

22. Ibid., p. 4.

23. Quoted in *Chronicle of Higher Education,* February 5, 1973.

24. The best treatment of the organizational aspects of the higher education community remains Harland G. Bloland, *Higher Education Associations in a Decentralized Education System* (Center for Research and Development in Higher Education, University of California, Berkeley, 1969).

25. Quoted in the *Chronicle of Higher Education,* October 30, 1972.

26. Heyns, "The National Higher Educational Establishment," p. 160.

27. Heyns, "The National Higher Educational Establishment," p. 162.

6

The Prospects for Higher Education in National Politics

Higher Education as a Developing Interest Group

In little more than a decade, higher education has moved from the fringes of national politics to become a major claimant on national resources and good will. Central to this transformation has been the greatly enhanced social, economic, and political expectations associated with specialized learning in the knowledgeable society.[a] This discussion has concentrated on the response of higher education to these changes by focusing on the Washington representatives, those who reflect one aspect of higher education as a developing interest group.

The characteristics of a group moving from a nascent to developing interest status include: (1) the creation of structures and institutions within the interest group and government that facilitate or inhibit the political prospects for the group; (2) the transformation in staffing these new organizations from those with little political experience to those displaying some savvy and experience in national politics; (3) growing concern for the most effective and appropriate ways to defend and promote the group's interests and (4) the general absence of extensive and reliable contacts within the executive and legislative branches.

The speed with which higher education moved into the status of a developing interest group is indicated by a number of signs. For example, it was not until 1960 that higher education was able to offer an alternative proposal for the college construction program pressed by the Eisenhower administration. By 1961 higher education had forged a coalition around a combined loan and grant program for classroom construction with a specific formula for the two types of support based on a careful survey of institutional requirements. By 1963 the American Council had expanded

---

[a] For example, consumer advocate Ralph Nader's Project on Corporate Responsibility tried to enlist major university stockholders in the General Motors Corporation to exert pressures on the company to be more responsive to public interests in pollution and safety. Democratic Senator Lee Metcalf of Montana charged that the nation's most prestigious universities failed to try to influence the racial, environmental, safety, and pricing policies of business corporations in which they owned sizable blocks of voting stock. He argued that "universities could perform monumental service to their country at a critical point in its history by redirection of the voting power of university stock." Quoted in the *Hartford Times,* December 29, 1970.

its federal relations staff and had begun to set up a fairly efficient communications network between member campuses and the Washington office.

The posture of higher education toward politics at the beginning of the decade was captured in a memorandum addressed to questions about the political organization of higher education. In late 1960 the executive secretaries and elected heads of a dozen major national organizations convened to explore the questions, "Is higher education properly organized to get *all* it should?" and "Is higher education properly organized to get the *kind* of assistance it *wants?*" A background memorandum considering these questions argued that there were "undeniable weaknesses in the present system," and that the American Council's Committee on Relationships of Higher Education to the Federal Government,

> while quite competent through knowledge and experience to devise policies in the best interest of higher education, can bring little pressure to bear on constituent organizations, which sometimes take positions on Federal legislation after general discussion at annual meetings without the benefit of the detailed staff work essential to fully informed judgments. On numerous occasions the show of near unanimity by representatives of national organizations in Congressional committee hearings has been achieved by presenting testimony in such a way as to minimize differences clearly on the record. This much can be achieved by agreement among the executive secretaries; but frequently it is not enough. There is need for closer year-round liaison among the major educational organizations on Federal legislative issues.[1]

In addition to the absence of regular, close contacts among the major associations, there were other problems as well. There were few established contacts among the various interests and no regular or predictable patterns of contact with government agencies and potential allies outside or inside the higher education community. Moreover, there were no identifiable groups of lobbyists or political professionals distinct from the executive secretaries.

The changes that occurred in the Washington higher education community through the 1960s were rarely the product of initiatives taken by the association representatives, but were instead responses to new federal policies and to constituent pressures. At the heart of the changes were structural and organizational modifications and transformations. These included the proliferation of representatives from different parts of higher education; the creation of informal and quasi-formal structures for promoting common interests; the rise of a cadre of political specialists; and the shift in significant policy-making responsibility from association membership to more politically knowledgeable and sensitive representatives based in Washington.

Proliferation of Washington Representatives

The increased availability of categorical funds for scientific research and specific programs prompted the rapid growth in the number of Washington offices supported by individual schools, small associations, and state systems. College administrators wishing to take advantage of the programs felt that the existing multipurpose associations were incapable of providing the kinds of liaison between granting agencies and individual institutions that were crucial for obtaining program support.

The proliferation of offices outside the orbit of the established major associations had three important effects. First, it provided a highly visible acknowledgment that colleges and universities had responded to the rapidly changed relationship between higher education and the federal government. Second, it helped jolt the complacency of the established associations and prompted them to establish their own federal relations programs and to reassess their efforts in legislative relations. Finally, although the small offices lacked the staff, time, and money to play a sustained political role, they did have the kinds of homogeneous memberships and independence of movement that made it possible for them to establish independent pockets of influence with state delegations and to act as critics of the established associations. Table 6–1 shows the rapidity with which the major components of the Washington higher education community developed during the 1960s.

Changes in the Structures for
Promoting Common Interests

Basic to the evolution of a coherent and identifiable pattern of policy and decision making in the Washington community have been changes in the structures for collective and cooperative action. The multiplication of representatives throughout the 1960s has diminished the importance of the bimonthly Governmental Relations Luncheon Group and encouraged the transfer of strategic policy discussions to the restricted confines of the Secretariat and the coordinating council set up by Roger Heyns. The Secretariat, first convened regularly in 1962, marked the first formal effort at creating a regular point of policy and strategic exchange among the executive secretaries of the major and several minor associations. Although there is an explicit recognition that the political interests of the various members of the higher education community do differ, there exists what amounts to a community norm that associations leaders keep each other informed about all important political activities and policy positions. The

Table 6–1

The Development of Washington Representation

Association or Office	Founded	Membership	Washington Office Opened	Federal Program Began
Major Associations				
National Association of State Universities and Land-Grant Colleges	1887[a]	130	1947	1947
Association of American Colleges	1915	779	1947	1968
Association of American Universities	1900	50[b]	1962	1969
American Association of State Colleges and Universities	1961	314	1962	1967
American Association of Community and Junior Colleges	1920	875	1939	1965
American Council on Education	1918	1,399[c]	1918	1962
Special-Purpose Associations				
Association of American Medical Colleges	1876	111[d]	1965	1970
Council of Graduate Schools	1960	324	1962	1962
Council of Protestant Colleges and Universities	1958	230[e]	1960	None
Council for the Advancement of Small Colleges	1956	140	1956	None
American Association of Colleges of Teacher Education	1917	863	1959	1969
Small Associations and State Systems				
College and University Division, National Catholic Education Association		228	1929	
State Colleges of South Dakota		6	1965	1965
University of California		9	1960	1960
State Colleges of California		19	1968	1968
Association of Jesuit Colleges and Universities[f]		28	1962	1962
Division of Educational Services of the Lutheran Council		44	1967	1967
Associated Colleges of the Midwest		12	1966	1966
East Central College Consortia		7	1968	1968
College Service Bureau		114	1969	1969

[a] Founded as the Association of State Universities and Land-Grant Colleges.
[b] Includes two Canadian institutions.
[c] Institutional members, 1974.
[d] Includes 16 Canadian institutions.
[e] Disbanded, 1970.
[f] Until 1970, Jesuit Education Association.

monthly meeting of the Secretariat provides an opportunity for these kinds of exchanges. Its participants, however, still do not accord it sufficient stature and legitimacy to institutionalize it to the point where it can impose sanctions on its members.

A New Cadre of Political Specialists

The Washington representatives comprise a growing cadre of political specialists that is the direct consequence of the proliferating desire for representation by all parts of postsecondary education. Over the decade recruitment of representatives has placed decreasing stress upon academic measures of promise and prestige. More and more stress has been placed on prior experience and knowledge about the intricacies of national politics. For the most part the representatives are specialists in the compilation and dissemination of political intelligence. Increasingly, however, they are responsible for integrating the interest positions of their constituents with their own professional evaluations of the political strengths and liabilities of different courses of action. They are compelled by their shared address at One Dupont Circle to keep up the diplomatic skills that are so necessary for representing their constituents' interests to the government, as well as to different parts of the education community. Their numbers are still small. No association maintains more than three persons who by the most inclusive definition can be considered political operators (in comparison to the American Farm Bureau Federation, for example, which has eight registered lobbyists looking out for its interests). The important point for the development of higher education as a national interest is that higher education now has the services of an increasingly experienced group of pragmatically inclined political operatives that did not exist as a discernible group until the late 1960s.

Shift in Policy-Making Responsibility

Another important indicator of higher education's political evolution has been the subtle, at times imperceptible, shift in decision making out of the hands of the college administrators and into the hands of the politically knowledgeable staffs that man the Washington offices. The kind of policy immobilization caused by an ideologically motivated minority over the federal aid issue in the early 1960s is far less likely to occur than it was a decade ago. The frustrations over the initial federal aid controversy, particularly over the inability to present a coherent position on aid, caused a precipitous decline in the importance attached to regular surveys of rank-

and-file positions on policy issues. In the place of participatory policy making there has been a tendency toward the formulation of policy positions by the appropriate association board or commission in close consultation with federal relations specialists.

The rise of a politically competent group of representatives and the rapid turnover of college executives, most of whom have severely limited understanding and experience with Washington politics, have encouraged a new generation of college presidents to entrust at least tactical decisions to their men in Washington.

The Prospects for Washington Representation and Higher Education in Politics

Higher education's strong identification as a distinctive area of American education has been reflected in a long history of associational ties and activities. Until the early 1960s, however, associational contacts rarely included intense political concerns and only limited collective political self-consciousness. The growth and increasingly professional character of Washington representation is an important sign of the transformation from the casual exchanges of a nascent interest group, to the heightened political self-consciousness, the increased regularity of cooperation between organizations and to the increasingly experienced cadre of political specialists characteristic of a developing interest group. It is unlikely, however, that higher education will move toward the status of a mature, well-established national interest group with anything like the speed that marked its initial entrance into national politics. Instead, the prospects are for the persistence of a style based primarily on consultation rather than negotiation, for limited changes in the structure of the Washington higher education community, and for continued ambivalence over the propriety and legitimacy of more explicit involvement in the mechanics of political decision making.

Where negotiation is the distinctive characteristic of policy making, it is the government that shapes policy, contingent upon the actual approval of interested parties, thus giving the affected interest at least the chance to veto impending decisions. In contrast, when consultation characterizes policy making, the views of the organization are solicited and taken into account but not considered by policy makers to be in any sense decisive.[2] At the heart of the distinction is an explicit or implicit acknowledgment by political decision makers that the interested group or organization has sufficient political power and influence to seriously restrict government options for unilateral or decisive action. The consultation pattern seeks to incorporate the views and opinions of the affected group but is based on the assumption that the group does not have enough political clout to do any real damage to decision makers. Thus, they feel relatively uninhibited about acting independently of the group's expressed policy positions.

The consultative style has been the characteristic pattern of political relationships between higher education and government. For example, higher education has been remarkably dependent upon the personalities of the secretary of Health, Education, and Welfare, a situation that reflects the general absence of a close clientele relationship in this key department. Educators felt that while Abraham Ribicoff was the head of HEW under the Kennedy administration he quickly alienated the education community by refusing to recognize the legitimacy of education's claims. The feelings toward Commissioner of Education Sterling McMurrin, under Ribicoff, were ambiguous, but most educators seemed to feel that his authority was circumscribed by Ribicoff. In contrast, Washington representatives felt that McMurrin's successor, Francis Keppel of Harvard, shared their perspectives and had the political skills necessary to communicate them within the Kennedy administration and the Congress.[3]

There are several reasons that the consultative style will probably persist in the political relations of higher education and government. In the first place, higher education has been habituated to the more passive role in the government-higher education partnership. The producer-consumer relationship that has for so long been the predominant pattern between the federal government and higher education is just beginning to shift toward a more general concern for the institutional welfare of higher education. The new trend in federal policy is for a changed pattern of federal support that does not submerge higher education's priorities under federal priorities, but that is designed to assist institutions in meeting their own missions as well as those of national or federal interests.[4] Concrete manifestations of actions taken by higher education and the Nixon administration point up the new direction in federal policy. In the spring of 1971 the American Council along with six other major associations argued that rapidly escalating costs, cutbacks in federal and state support, and rising enrollments had combined to make a program of institutional support vital. At the same time the Nixon administration abandoned its earlier unwillingness to propose any general program of aid to institutions and began working on an institutional plan that would provide colleges and universities with general-purpose funds. Higher education pressure for generalized institutional support is the first significant departure since the Higher Education Facilities Act of 1963 to place an overwhelming emphasis on a policy so clearly benefiting colleges and universities and minimizing the consumer relationship with the government.

More concretely, higher education is still not organized to play a more assertive role, in spite of the changes that have occurred over the past decade. Structure is critical for the development of a negotiative style.

Genuine and legitimate negotiations can take place only if governmental decision-making processes and patterns of action within interest groups enable those who speak for government and those who speak for the interest group to commit those whom they represent.[5] For higher education to develop a negotiative style, it would be necessary to concentrate authority at some point within the higher education establishment. The response of most Washington representatives to the Sullivan proposal indicates that it is highly unlikely that they would endorse the kinds of discretionary authority necessary for the conduct of binding negotiations.

It does not appear that steps have been taken that might modify these organizational deficiencies. Daniel P. Moynihan, former counselor to President Nixon, challenged college administrators to organize themselves better to influence government policy on the support of higher education. Speaking at the 1970 annual meeting of the American Council on Education, he asserted that "if there is to be fundamental reform in the relations between the national government and higher education, there will have to be leadership on both sides; there will have to be negotiations, agreement, oversight, revision. The higher education community is not now organized for any such effort. It has no such men. It seemingly comprehends no such undertakings." [b]

Senator Pell, chairman of the subcommittee on education, angrily attacked the Washington higher education associations as uncooperative and resistant to new ideas. As noted above, he was particularly distressed about the failure of the major associations to pay attention to higher education developments in the Senate or to assist in the drafting of legislation, and stated that:

It appeared that the higher education community was ignoring what was going on in the Senate. Interest and contact seemed to me minimal. The failure of that community to perceive what was occurring in the Senate caused my staff to advise the higher education community that they should rethink their position on institutional aid so that, if institutional aid were adopted, they would not be left out in the cold.[6]

In addition to habits of passivity, and organizational deficiencies, higher education has yet to utilize fully the full range of potential political resources at its command. Professional lobbyists become especially frustrated

---

[b] Quoted in *Chronicles of Higher Education,* October 19, 1970. In an interview after his speech, Moynihan conceded that leaders of the higher education community "have an awful problem. They are living under siege with no national cohesion and caught between a hostile public and the students. They are in desperate financial condition. And they are not going to get anything out of Congress without some allies. They've been so fractured that they [do not have] a decent presence in Washington."

at what they perceive as higher education's failure to exploit its rich resources for political objectives. One lobbyist representing the book publishing interests stressed the critical lack of political sophistication and commitment on the part of higher education during the full-funding battle.

I just don't feel they see their stakes as clearly as they should in the political process. They have real power, but they just don't use it. There are colleges in nearly every congressional or senatorial district, so it should be possible to mobilize the administrators, particularly the presidents and trustees and have them get in touch with the representatives. These schools should get in touch with alumni who are on the Hill. They should direct some money towards their friends at election time, and not just show up when it's time to testify.

The point is that higher education offers very little to the political decision maker to compensate for the services expected of him by higher education. It does not appear that higher education has devoted serious consideration to ways to assist its supporters at election time although evidence from this study is negligible on this point. Although the University of Texas system's Washington office shut down after about two years, one of its main tasks was to provide staff assistance to the Texas delegation, thus providing the one resource that exists in plenty—expert knowledge on a wide variety of subjects.

By trying to translate professionalism and expertise into political currency, the Texas system sought to make an investment in future political access. Although the evaluation and use of political resources is particularly critical at a time when two of higher education's traditional resources, public good will and presidential and institutional prestige, have been eroded by student unrest and rapid presidential turnovers, few offices have made serious, systematic efforts to take inventories of their political resources.

There are also structural and ideological features in government that encourage the persistence of the consultative style. Ideologically, there is a strong tendency for decision makers to adopt a trustee posture toward higher education, one in which they take on roles as guardians of the public interest in education. Such a role removes education—at least symbolically—from interest politics and elevates it to a plane that transcends the normal operations of other interest groups. In effect, education is far too important to be left to the educators. For example, the recent Carnegie Commission on Higher Education (as well as several earlier government task forces) were notable for their exclusion of members of the Washington higher education establishment. The sharp reactions of certain legislators to higher education's association with the Full-Funding Committee reflected their expectations that the political activities of higher education should be conducted in a restrained manner that was far more appropriate for the stature of the educational enterprises. These perspectives and expectations of policy makers are hardly conducive to an interest group's efforts to infiltrate the policy process in a way that creates fairly permanent and predictable clientele relationships critical for the development of a negotiative style.

Structurally, the newness of most higher education policies has also militated against the creation of firm clientele relationships that are characteristic of more mature interests. Higher education still lacks the range and diversity of contacts throughout the legislative and bureaucratic structure that characterizes interest groups like agriculture, business, or labor.

Just as any dramatic shifts in the government-higher education relationship are unlikely, there are few prospects for any substantial changes in the existing infrastructure of the Washington higher education community. The offices designed to function as liaisons between institutions and granting agencies will probably remain fairly constant in their grantsman roles and numbers as the shift from categorical, programmatic aid to more general support takes place. Educational entrepreneurs will come and go but in far fewer numbers than at the peak of higher education legislation and appropriations during the mid-1960s. The money that feeds the profit motives of the entrepreneurial representatives during times of tight budgets is hardly enough incentive to make representation of specific schools especially appealing. Those businessmen likely to remain in the representation field will be those with multipurpose organizations that handle public relations and fund-raising and extend no effort to make their operations dependent upon college representation. In any event, these kinds of profit-making operations have lacked the scope and legitimacy to play any but the most marginal political role.

The Washington offices of the state systems, small associations, and individual schools (as well as the commuter representatives) are likely to be fairly permanent fixtures in the Washington community. It is unlikely that they will expand the way they did throughout the past decade unless there is a significant reversion to categorical support or increased funding for existing programs. The hazards for these small offices stem from the same financial pressures and uncertainties that plague the institutions themselves. The operations of the Washington offices are vulnerable items on institutional budgets, particularly the state offices that have been unable to convince frugal and skeptical state legislators about the value of the Washington outpost. Individual schools are also likely to see the Washington office as a luxury that they can ill-afford when other parts of the institution's programs are suffering elimination or cutbacks.

The political roles and impact of the state, small association, and individual school offices will be not significantly different from what they have been since their openings in the middle and late 1960s. Their limited resources and manpower will continue to limit the actual political activities in which they might become involved. They still, however, have enough flexibility and access to establish limited but direct contacts with state delegations and actively support specific efforts like full funding. They will provide additional sources of political information and intelligence. In addition, the more aggressive representatives in these offices can still prod, criticize, and cajole the more complacent established associations and continue to challenge the assumptions that justify the existing status quo. More typically, however, these representatives will continue to work primarily as liaisons between government and campus and are likely to place increased emphasis on their service functions as the political initiative slips back to the major associations.

The most important consequence of the shift from categorical to general student aid or limited institutional support by the federal government will be to increase the burden of political activity in the major associations. They have the resources, the experienced political specialists, and the organized constituencies to maintain sustained political efforts. For example, in the recurrent discussions of the various positions on federal aid to higher education, fuller funding of existing legislation, new programs of student aid for the disadvantaged, student loan banks, and general or institutional support plans, it becomes clear that the key variable for support by congressional and executive decision makers is the existence of a visible, organized constituency. The two legislative proposals that made the most headway in 1971 were those relating to institutional support and the Community College Act. Enthusiastic and sustained support for student loan banks and Nixon administration emphasis on loans to low-income students was almost totally lacking. One experienced Washington representative concluded that the most potent political force for higher education in Washington in early 1970 was that which sought fuller funding of existing programs.

This constituency, represented by the associations and their member colleges, probably has more strength and unity than ever before, and powerful allies in other educational associations, the labor movement, and in Congress. . . . The constituency is united around the importance of full funding. It does not give . . . much attention . . . to the problems of student aid or the disadvantaged. In part, this may be a reflection of political realities, what Congress will buy, where the allies are. *In part . . . it is because neither the student aid forces nor spokesmen for higher education of the disadvantaged are well enough organized to make their cases effectively, to the associations, Congress, or the executive branch.*[7]

The more fundamental implication of the shift in forms of federal support, be it increased funding for authorized programs or a new policy of generalized institutional or student support, means that there will be no diminution of higher education's political stakes. An increased federal presence in the financing of higher education automatically means deeper involvement in the political process, and more specifically, in the appropriations process. In short, higher education will try to get more money while defending what it already has. The problem is, however, that any generalized form of federal support is vulnerable to political and budgetary considerations over which specific interests like higher education have little or no control. For example, student-aid funds for 1972 were only two-thirds of the authorized amount. Complicating this failure to fund the student-aid programs fully were increased enrollments, plus the fact that 250 additional institutions were competing for what was about the same amount of money as in the preceding year. The point is that the allocation of federal money is a political matter subject to grave uncertainties and tough competition from all quarters.

The question then becomes the way in which higher education will respond to the implications of the expanded federal interest. The only prospect for a significant departure is in the erosion of higher education's isolation from other compatible interests in the pursuit of similar goals. The appropriations process, compared with the policy-making process, is far more susceptible to broad-based coalition efforts, as indicated by the Full-Funding Committee. Although most of the higher education representatives would look askance at the prospects of logrolling, it is conceivable that higher education could forge alliances with interests like elementary-secondary education, science and health lobbies, and certain welfare movements with educational implications, on appropriations issues. The catalyst for participation in such activities is not likely to come from within the higher education community as it is now constituted, but will have to come from the outside, as it did in full funding. The likelihood that higher education will offer its support to such efforts will in turn be in direct proportion to its anticipated financial stakes.

Aside from the possibility for increased cooperative efforts outside the immediate higher education community, the changes that take place in the political life of the associations will be in magnitude and scope, not fundamental shifts in organization or involvement. There will continue to be stepped up activity in three areas: intelligence and information-gathering; diplomatic efforts at building and maintaining the essential integrity of the higher education community; and the recruitment of representatives with particular skills and experience in politics. Increased emphasis on these areas will be the product of increased support to the legislative relations activities of the major associations, a move that can be accomplished with a fairly modest shift in association resources. It must be kept in mind, however, that although the major associations have made definite moves to enhance their legislative and federal relations work, these activities still make up a small part of association services and activities.

The painful experience of the battle over the 1972 amendments brought home to the educators the importance policy makers attach to the presentation of careful and thorough factual studies in support of legislative objectives. This experience has finally provided the impetus for more extensive data-gathering and closer cooperation with the institutional research offices of member colleges and universities, as indicated by the creation of the ACE Policy Analysis Service, and addition of expanded federal relations staffs in the AAU and the AASCU. Even the politically effective Land-Grant Association set up a separate office of Governmental Relations. The kinds of issues wrapped up in the financial situation of higher education are the kinds of issues that lend themselves especially well to quantitative and factual documentation. The necessity for the careful presentation of this kind of data takes on an added dimension when decision makers are also listening to testimony and reading studies conducted by specialists outside the higher education community. Several of the important policy studies relating to the financial crisis in higher education were conducted under the auspices of the Brookings Institution and the Carnegie Commission on Higher Education.[8] The point is that policy objectives are increasingly presented and challenged on grounds based on particular expertise in sociology, economics, or education, not on intuitive assessments or personal preferences of particular college presidents. Few members of the Washington community have yet embarked on the systematic exploitation of the expertise residing in their member institutions.

The two other changes likely to take place within the major associations are qualitative transitions that will be subtle and uneven; they will involve the recruitment of representatives with backgrounds and skills in Washington politics, and the increased importance attached to the diplomatic roles played by the representatives. Efforts to recruit men with knowledge and experience in the details of Washington policy making are one inevitable consequence of higher education's increased involvement with the federal government. Because the prospects are for further shifts in the direction of even more federal ties to higher education, it would be unrealistic and in some cases counterproductive for higher education to be represented by amateurs. Political representation is a role for professionals, a fact that higher education has come to recognize as reflected in the shifts toward younger, more politically experienced representatives in the Washington offices. One important signal in the regard is the appointment of Charles Saunders, former deputy assistant secretary for education in the Department of Health, Education and Welfare, to take over Jack Morse's job as director of ACE's federal relations operation.

The last significant change that is likely to take place in higher education representation, particularly that of the major associations, is an increased emphasis on the diplomatic arts of negotiation and compromise. These kinds of interpersonal skills will be necessary in maintaining the essential integrity of the higher education community in presenting unified political positions that contributed so much to the policy successes of the preceding decade. The tasks involved in sustaining this working unanimity are likely to be substantial, given the kinds of fault lines that continue to divide American higher education. For example, the interests of the small, private colleges are radically different from those of the large, research universities, many of which are publicly funded. The inexorably climbing costs of higher education have put the private colleges at a severe disadvantage in competition from lower-cost, publicly supported state colleges, universities, and community colleges. Collective data from the public and private sectors of higher education indicate that the private component has declined proportionately to the public institutions in terms of the number of schools, enrollment, and degrees granted at all levels. The percentage of total enrollment in private higher education has plunged from 50 per cent in the fall of 1949 to just 23 per cent in the fall of 1972.[9] There are also potential conflicts inherent in the different objectives of graduate and undergraduate programs, and the contrasting styles and objectives of traditional elitist higher education and the growing constituency for vocational and community college education. These areas of real and potential conflict are far from exhaustive. They merely illustrate that special skills and patience will be necessary to seek out common interests, to minimize overt conflicts, and to act whenever feasible in cooperative fashion.

Any significant changes beyond these kinds of increases in scope and emphasis within the major associations are extremely unlikely for several reasons. The most basic one is that any new organizational structure or mechanism devoted exclusively to political representation would be an intolerable challenge to the prevailing status quo and the existing distribution of power and influence. The policy crisis for higher education is not yet so acute that the representatives of the individual associations are ready to submerge their own competitive advantages in collective efforts of uncertain quality and effect. They still remain fiercely jealous of their independence and flexibility, in spite of their willingness to seek out areas of compromise. In addition, many representatives have an implicit disdain for the tedious mechanics of the political process itself. This sentiment is reinforced by the feeling that an assertive political role is neither legitimate nor compatible with the comportment of those associated with the higher learning. In a more immediate sense, inhibitions stemming from questions of tax status further complicate the prospects for substantial change in the direction of more explicit, assertive political behavior.

It is misleading, however, to suggest that either the representatives or the associations themselves are behaving in some selfish, parochial manner in their unenthusiastic reaction to proposals for extensive changes in the existing framework of Washington representation. Because they are in fact representative of a broader constituency, it is their responsibility to represent their memberships in a way that is compatible with the desires of their clients while seeking to implement the general policies established by them. The Washington representatives are simply not autonomous; they cannot often take positions that exceed the expectations or desires of those whom they represent. Until there is movement for more assertive behavior and more effective mechanisms of interest articulation from the membership, it would border on the presumptuous and irresponsible for the Washington representatives to seek to engineer such changes themselves.

Notes

1. Quoted in Homer D. Babbidge, Jr. and Robert M. Rosenzweig, *The Federal Interest in Higher Education,* (New York: McGraw-Hill Book Company, 1962).

2. Harry Eckstein, *Pressure Group Politics: The Case of the British Medical Association* (Stanford: Stanford University Press, 1960), p. 23.

3. Lawrence K. Pettit, *The Politics of Federal Policy Making for Higher Education,* manuscript, chap. II, pp. 36–38.

4. Peter P. Muirhead, "The New Pattern of Federal Aid to Higher Education," *Educational Record* 50 (Spring 1969): 171–73.

5. Eckstein, *Pressure Group Politics,* p. 23.

6. Quoted in *Chronicle of Higher Education,* August 2, 1971.

7. John P. Mallan, "Current Proposals for Federal Aid to Higher Education: Some Political Implications," in Orwig, ed., *Financing Higher Education: Alternatives for the Federal Government,* p. 321. Emphasis added.

8. For example, see Carnegie Commission on Higher Education, *Quality and Equality: New Levels of Federal Responsibility for Higher Education* (Highstown, N.J.: McGraw-Hill, 1968); Earl F. Cheit, *The New Depression in Higher Education* (New York: McGraw-Hill, 1971); and Alice M. Rivlin and Jeffrey H. Weiss, "Social Goals and Federal Support of Higher Education: The Implications of Various Strategies," in U.S. Congress Joint Committee, *The Economics and Financing of Higher Education in the United States* (Washington, D.C.: U.S. Government Printing Office, 1969), pp. 543–55.

9. *Digest of Educational Statistics,* 1973, National Center for Educational Statistics, Office of Education, (U.S. Department of Health, Education and Welfare, Washington, D.C., 1974), p. 68.

Index

125

About the Author

Lauriston R. King received the B.A. from Tufts University and the Ph.D. in Political Science from the University of Connecticut in 1971. He spent a year as a Postdoctoral Fellow in the Marine Policy and Ocean Management Program of the Woods Hole Oceanographic Institution. Dr. King joined the Office for the International Decade of Ocean Exploration, National Science Foundation, in 1972 where he is now Special Assistant for Marine Science Affairs. He has authored or coauthored articles in *The Public Interest, Public Policy, Comparative Political Studies,* and *Change* magazine, as well as book reviews and review articles for *Polity* and *Perspective. The Washington Lobbyists for Higher Education* is his first book.